HAWAIIAN
STAR

HAWAIIAN STAR

CHET GRITZMACHER

Kekapress

Published in the United States by Kekapress
P O Box 270, Salt Lake City, Utah. 84110

Hawaiian Star ©

Library of Congress Control Number (LCCN): TXu 2-341-306
ISBN: 979-8-9871430-0-1

Chet Lewis Gritzmacher
P O Box 270
Salt Lake City, Utah 84110

chetgritzmacher@kekapress.com

For Brandon and my Hawaiian *Ohana*.

For my husband Peter,
gratitude for his constant support.

Kakou—We are one.

TABLE OF CONTENTS

The brightest star in the Hawaiian night sky is Sirius (**the Dog Star**). In Hawaii, it has many names but is commonly called A'a. Sirius passes directly over Tahiti and Polynesian navigators used it to find their way back to Hawaii. Located in constellation, Canis Major (the Large Dog), Sirius is its heart.

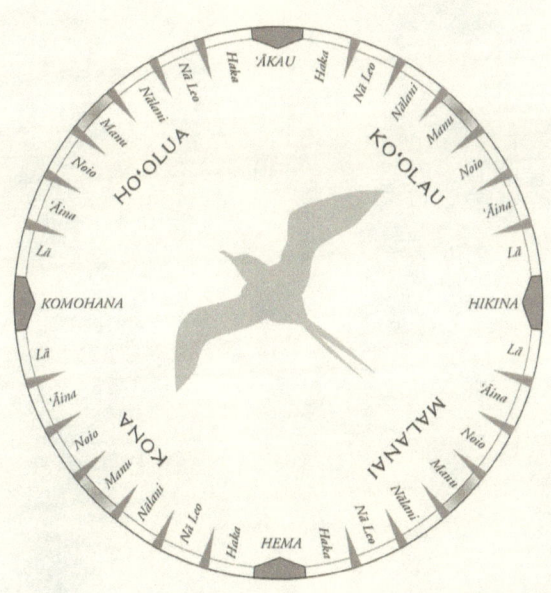

PROLOGUE

Sitting in the middle seat of the gigantic Boeing 747, I was about to begin a journey that would forever change the path of my life. I had a one way ticket to Honolulu, Hawaii. I was departing from Salt Lake City, Utah and I was not even keenly aware of where Hawaii was. I had faith that the $500 that I had in my pocket, a suitcase, and my bicycle in the cargo hold would take me forward into a life that I had not even contemplated. As the massive engines fired up and we began to speed down the runway, I silently knew that if this jumbo jet could take off, I too could take off into a world yet to be experienced. I was about to see what was on the other side of the pond.

"In the end we can only regret the chances we didn't take, and the relationships we were afraid to have, and the decisions that we waited too long to make." -Lewis Caroll

A hui hou...

Chapter One
"KA HOOMAKA ANA"
the beginning

*"It is impossible to live without failing at something,
unless you live so cautiously that you might as well
not have lived at all—in which case you fail by default."*

- J.K.ROWLING -

A new breeze was whisking across the fountain that was adjacent to University of Utah Business School. On this day in May, my wandering soul was awakening to a spirit that was being carried aloft on the wings of the wind. I sat with my back to the cascading water and I looked bemusedly at the emerald green valley below. The blooming spring was bringing the smiles of an ever joyful mother nature. It was a good time for me to stop and sit still and listen. I would soon hear breezes from a whole other universe begin to whisper.

This was the end of my last semester of my four-year full ride scholarship. The graduating class of 1974 would not have me in its lineup. I simply had not met the requirements for graduation. I was unable to raise the anchor that held the knowledge that education would open paths for a better life. I knew this would be an unhappy announcement that I would soon have to make to my father. I could hear his voice in my head as he would repeatedly say to me.

"Son all you need to do is to get your sheep's skin and you can do anything."

Fortunately for the animal, no dead ruminant would have to lose its skin for my benefit. I had recently read that the last year a college in the United States had awarded a sheepskin diploma was in 2019. The reactions of many of the students interviewed in the article said that they felt a little bit of betrayal and that those traditions mattered. I wondered how that got by animal rights activists for such a long time? I knew that my failure in not gaining a sheep skin diploma, or otherwise paper, was not fatal to either myself or the sheep.

I worked at the First Security Bank as a teller during my time at University. The Assistant Manager Mr. McNair was sure that I would be the next great shining star to be accepted into the bank's management training program after I graduated. He would speak *at* me but not *to* me as he repeated the same phrase: "Motivation and training will take you up the ladder to success, young man."

He was a short pudgy man and in answering I had to look down at him standing there in his dark gray suit, which he wore every day, and attempt to smile and answer.

"Yes sir, I said, I am grateful for that opportunity."

This fine day, I seemed to have a sense of peace knowing that the path from graduation and up the ladder of success in the training program would not be happening.

I went into work early and I entered the employee lounge to await my 12 noon starting time. Fellow tellers Shiela, Jackie, and Paul were sitting at one of the lunch tables and they seemed hushed in their conversation. I moved my chair a bit closer to their table to capture bits of their discussion of flying to Hawaii. I boldly jumped into the conversation and said, "Are you going to Hawaii?"

Paul looked up at me and said, "Yes, not only are we going to Hawaii, we are going to be giving our two-week notices today, we are are leaving Small Lake City and moving to Paradise."

I was definitely not a part of their circle of friendship and yet I freely asked, "Can I go with you?"

My request seemed to jump out of me without any cerebral thought whatsoever. They all looked at me like a puppy cocking their heads to the side, as if they did not hear me. "Say that again" was circling around in the back of their minds. Jackie kindly answered back. "Please join us tonight at my apartment, we are going to discuss the details of our trip and what we need to accomplish before we leave."

She wrote down her address and handed it to me.

"I'm happy that you have an interest in joining us, said Jackie, see you at 6 pm."

❀ ❀ ❀ ❀ ❀

As the hands on the clock moved forward to signify closing time, I anxiously summoned the Bank branch manager to assist me in my designated daily task of closing the vault. He too thought that I would soon be joining the white-shirt-tie squad of the Bank Management Training program. I was keenly aware of an immediate sense of joy that if I quit, I would not have to ride in the elevator with the manager and push a trolley full of money down to the cellar of the bank each night. I had an intense fear of elevators, and a greater fear of the potential of a bank robber that may be lurking in the cellar. I feared that he would lock me in the vault after stealing the money and saying *"Aloha"* even before I could consider leaving for paradise. As we entered the elevator, I remembered a nightmare that I walked into the elevator as a twenty-year old and I looked into the mirror and I had become an old man. That will definitely not be happening to me in my future.

❀ ❀ ❀ ❀ ❀

When I arrived at Jackie's apartment they had all consumed a couple of glasses of wine. I was offered a glass and I graciously declined stating that I was driving, leaving out the fact that I was not yet 21. I was unaware at that time, that the legal drinking age in Hawaii was 18. I would soon become an adult the minute I landed in paradise in so many unanticipated ways. I thanked Jackie for inviting me and briefly apologized for my butting in on their conversation.

"No worries," she said. Paul continued with his story.

"I graduated from the University of Utah last year and I went instantly into the Management Training Program at the bank. I've been unhappy with my path of becoming a banker. I have a sister who lives in Hawaii and she has suggested that I follow suit and move there as well."

Jackie piped in and said, "I have worked at bank for ten years as an administrative assistant to the bank manager. I have never been offered an advancement and my future as a woman working in a Mormon-owned, male-dominated bank was at a dead end."

She was happy to accept Paul's invitation to go along with him. It was now Shielas turn to reveal her wishes for wanting to go to Hawaii. She said, "Jackie and I have become best friends at work. I had previously worked at an auto parts store and I fell in love with the parts manager. He managed to have an interest in parts of other girls at the same time as a love interest with me. I figured it was time for me to stop watering dead plants. I have decided to be like a tree and let the relationship leaves drop. I want to become a bright red hibiscus creating a new bloom every day, and not grieving for the bloom of yesterday. Hawaii is the place for me to begin to do that."

I instantly knew that Sheila was going to be a great companion on our mutual quest in searching out paradise. I felt strangely inadequate in my offerings and I said, "I just finished my last semester at the University of Utah. I do not have enough credits to graduate and this opportunity will give me a change of scenery and perhaps find what I didn't know that I was searching for. I am embarrassed to say, I don't know where Hawaii is. I have not even thought of the possibility of vacationing there let alone moving there! I am ready to open my eyes to new horizons, and I am going to join you with my eyes wide open. I am so happy that I am here now and soon on my way to somewhere new. Thank you all for including me."

❊ ❊ ❊ ❊ ❊

They shared with me a few requirements that were needed to go on this adventure that had been previously agreed upon.

- ONE month's living expense money
- ONE way airline ticket
- ONE bicycle
- ONE credit card

I had all of the Ones except for a credit card. There was no chance for that now as I too was planning on giving my two-week notice to the bank the following day. I reported to the group on my abilities to fulfill the requirements.

"I have $500 in cash and I think that should clearly get me through the few weeks that I will need to find a job. I have a bicycle and I am ready to purchase a one way ticket to Hawaii." It all sounded exactly as it should, a chance to go to Hawaii. I felt as if I had just won a trip on "Let's Make A Deal." This was my chance to cash in my lottery tickets and realize that I have already won. This adventure was my sudden wealth.

We agreed that we would leave on Memorial Day, Monday May 27, 1974. We made a call to Pan American Airlines and four center coach seats on the nonstop flight from San Francisco to Honolulu, Hawaii were reserved. We toasted to our future in Paradise and I left knowing that I was ready to accept the Hawaiian phrase that I would soon learn, "To live my life while the sun shines" —*Oi kau ka lau, E hana I ola Honau"*— and that sun would be shining down on me in Hawaii.

❋ ❋ ❋ ❋ ❋

The details of my preparations to leave seemed to already be in play. My lease was up and my roommate had secured other living arrangements. I was going to have to move anyway, so why not move to an exotic island with four strangers. I did have anxieties in having to tell my parents. I knew that it would be very hard for me to leave them and especially my mother. We have always had a special understanding of the love that we have for each other. My mother's stroke had left her with very limited speech at a young age, but we had the conversation of love and caring within our souls and hearts.

She understood me in a non-verbal way. I drove out to my small home town of Tooele, Utah to say goodbye for now to my family. In small towns, our companions are chosen for us and I seemed to have had very few chosen for me. I had just chosen a small group of strangers as my new traveling companions, or perhaps we had chosen each other.

My father was out in the chicken coop feeding his pheasants. He had invested his retirement time in raising these beautiful and yet somewhat mean birds. He had pock marks on his legs from being attacked by a few brutal roosters. I avoided going near the coops, not only because of the mean birds, but because of the plethora of mice that would feed themselves right along the pheasants. He saw that I had arrived and he came back to the house. I said, "Dad I need to tell you and mom something. I am going to be moving to Hawaii in two weeks."

He looked at me quizzically, as if one of the pheasants was pecking at his legs and said, "That is a long ways away."

I responded the best I could think of.

"Dad I actually don't know how far away it is, I don't even know where the Hawaiian Islands are."

He had a forced smile that just barely revealed the gold inlay in one of his front teeth. There seemed to be a sparkle from the inlay that reflected back at me, and I knew that he understood my wanderlust. My mother was silent but she had a sense of understanding in her eyes of my need at that time for an adventure. I did not have a lot of convincing to do for my sister Vickie to agree to take care of my car. I didn't even know if I could have a car in Hawaii, so that was it—it was not an ending but a beginning, not a goodbye— but a see you later.

Chapter Two
"E KOMI MAI"
welcome friends

"*Aloha* and welcome to Honolulu, local time is 3:45 pm and the outside temperature is 82 degrees." Those words said by the PanAm Stewardess were music to my ears. The goddesses of the skies had created a great experience at 30,000 feet. We were given a generous, delicious lunch, and a drink cart was pushed down the aisles that had a steaming volcano on it that was filled with pineapple juice for us to partake. After all of that, we still had time for a full-length movie. A game was played to see who could guess the exact distance and time when we would be half way across the ocean. That was a silly game for me to play, as I had no clue where in the Pacific I was going and how far away it was from the mainland. The Stewardess continued her announcement.

"As you deplane, a '*Wiki Wiki*' shuttle will be waiting to take you to the baggage claim area. On behalf of PanAmerican and the entire crew, we welcome you to Hawaii and we bid you a pleasant trip and we look forward to seeing you on board again in the near future. *Aloha.*"

I certainly had no clue what a *wiki wiki* shuttle was. The shuttles we boarded had been put in place at the airport in 1970 to replace outdated buses that were hot and slow. The open-air shuttles were quick (*wiki wiki*) and allowed us to enjoy the scent of the Plumeria trees as we approached the terminal. The magic of *Aloha* was immediate as I received my orchid lei from a striking Hawaiian *Wahine*. Will Rogers once said, "Hawaii is the only place I know where they lay flowers on you while you are alive." I felt that my life had gone from black and white to technicolor. The extremely large Boeing 747s were parked at the gates that appeared to be in the front yard of the airport, and the airport had no windows. I had an immediate sensation that I had arrived at my new home.

We collected our luggage and removed our bicycles from the boxes that were provided by the airline. We went to the curb for transportation to Waikiki without thinking that all of us would not fit in just one vehicle. A minor obstacle was soon resolved by two Filipino drivers who crammed everything into a couple of old American cars. They looked like old yellow cabs that may have been imported from New York City. Off we went to our first destination, the Waikiki Grand Hotel.

This small town boy had arrived at this international destination and to a beautiful hotel located only half a block from Waikiki Beach. The ten-story hotel overlooked Kapiolani Park, with sweeping views of the Diamond Head Volcano and the deep blue Pacific Ocean. The large open-air lobby beckoned our weary bodies with a scent of the ocean and sweet-sounding Hawaiian music. Large vases filled with heliconia, bird of paradise, anthuriums, and orchids sat on round tables throughout the lobby. The perfection of the flowers led me to believe that they certainly could not be real. Certainly not the case. Racks of pamphlets lined the walls, offering every tropical adventure imaginable. The desk clerk looked at us and said, "You all stay in one room? A very tight squeeze you know. Maybe mo better two rooms?"

His pidgin English was a new tone that none of us had heard before. Two short weeks ago I worked with these fellow travelers who I have only briefly known, and I would now be sleeping close to all of them and in the same room. No shame in that I thought. I was certain that these strangers were just my friends who were waiting to happen. It has been said that the fastest way to make a friend for life is to travel with a stranger. I was hopeful for that outcome.

I had to leave the check-in desk to go to the rest room. I saw two doors, one said *Kane*, the other said *Wahine*. I was fortunate to think that I knew that *Wahine* was a woman—I would at least have a 50/50 chance of being right. As I was washing my hands, in walked this very large person. I was a bit startled as I wasn't sure if I was seeing a man or a woman. The person was about 300 pounds, and had a pony tail bun on top of its head. Also strangely enough it looked as if this person was wearing a diaper. I was doubtful of having chosen the correct bathroom. I would later learn that this person was a Sumo wrestler. His hair was tied into a topknot and his diaper was essentially a thick 30-foot-long belt that was tied into knots to cover his particular body parts. I said to myself, Toto I don't think I'm in Utah any longer.

I had to take a quick walk outside and put my feet in the sand and anoint myself in the ocean. I made the sign of the cross and kissed my fingers and I looked up to the sky and saw an infinite amount of stars. Hawaii is the only place in the 50 states where you can see the stars of the entire northern and southern hemispheres. The Hawaiian star had safely guided me to the islands and to my new home.

❀ ❀ ❀ ❀ ❀

The exotic sounds from the animals at the Kapiolani Zoo started at the first glimmer of light. Huge Banyan trees prevented me from seeing the animals that were waking up with the sun. My senses were like the end of a lit sparkler jumping up into the sky. I jumped out of bed, while my traveling companions were still sleeping off their jet lag. The lobby of the hotel smelled of freshly brewed coffee with the scents of flowers as the sweetener. I grabbed a fresh cup and I headed the half block to Waikiki beach.

How could I have guessed as I walked onto the sand that this must be what Gulliver felt like as he traveled the world, as he returned with his stories of wonder, sharing stories of the beginning and ending with the experiences of his own legend. This was the beginning of my experience. My arms and legs were loosely attached to my body. The sights that I was experiencing were as if I was looking through a kaleidoscope of visions on a color wheel. This was my own 3-D view-master coming to life. I was entering a new world where I could be anything and experience it all. The inherent magic that was captured in 3D with the view-master was now right before my eyes. This was no postcard. I was experiencing the sights of this isolated jewel here in the middle of the vastness of the Pacific Ocean. I had grace in my step, a song in my mind, and a new found *Aloha* in my heart. The trade winds were bringing in visions of the future and preserving the cherished memories of the past.

As I walked along the beach, the early risers were setting up their spots along the white sandy beaches. The surfers were out in the warm waters, waiting for the waves to roll high. I only needed to walk in the sand along the ocean to feel the power of the universe and my closeness to the one who created it. The beauty of the ocean refusing to stop kissing the shore no matter how many times it swept the waves away was my natural pendulum of life in action.

I walked past beautiful bodies laying in the early morning sun. I had thoughts that I could only share with myself. The presence of so many beautiful men before my eyes was something that I had not prepared myself for. They looked so good, my eyes were seeing what my soul was not ready to explore. They were lying on the sand like sins in bathing suits. It seemed that there was an unreasonable quantity of male beauty right before my eyes. I immediately felt uncomfortable in my pressed shorts and collared shirt. My white legs surely announced the *haole*, "not native," that had just landed on the islands. I retreated from the beach bound to quickly take care of the fashion problem. I entered the first ABC convenience store that I saw. The store was clearly invented for the tourists and they sold the *"Aloha* wear" that I thought I should have. I felt that perhaps the more *Aloha* print that I could acquire, the happier I would be.

Chapter Three

"HE LA NANI KEA LA"
today is a beautiful day

A fresh morning breeze carried by the trade winds blew in from the shadows of Diamond Head. I was going to begin looking for our next place to call home. We were into day two at the hotel and day four would be check out time. Jackie, Shiela, and Paul headed to the beach with their towels, lotions, and baby oil as they did not seem the least bit concerned about where we would live. I was destined to find somewhere near where we could reside and begin our lives as islanders.

I walked to the local Star grocery market and purchased the Sunday section of the Honolulu Star Bulletin. I took the paper with me back to the *lanai* of the Hotel to begin circling listings that perhaps would be within the realm of possibilities. We had no steady income to rely on and no rental references of value to give a potential landlord. Somehow I did not think that looking for a house would be an obstacle, I saw it as a challenge, an opportunity of having a permanent Hawaiian address. I looked at each listing carefully and I only circled listings that were in Waikiki, that were affordable and were immediately available. After circling a limited amount of listings in the for-rent section that sounded somewhat promising, I moved on to the employment section. I thought that I had a feather in my pocket—I had a recommendation letter from the First Security Bank in Utah recommending me for a position in the banking field. Hope is a thing with feathers that perches in one's soul and is there for the picking, my feather was ready for the picking.

There were many listings for hotel positions, tour guides, and various tourism-related jobs. Near the end of the columns of openings was a listing that was the one for me, "Bank Teller at the Bank of Hawaii Airport Branch," applications would be accepted at any of the branch locations. There was something magical about this island, I was in a world that had is own fantasy, the magic was settling over me gently and clinging to me like pollen falling from the abundant fragrant flowers that were growing all around me.

I hurriedly put on the clothing that I had brought along for the purpose of a job interview. I felt certain that the white shirt and tie certainly would work for any available job opening.

I walked into the lobby of the Waikiki Grand and there was a new clerk at the desk. I greeted her. "Good morning can you guide me in the direction of a Bank of Hawaii?"

"There is one two blocks *Eva* and one block *Makai* on Kalakaua Avenue, right here in Waikiki," she replied.

Oh my I thought, this was not just Pidgin English I just heard, I had better look for a Hawaiian translation book. I walked out of the hotel and turned left onto Kuhio Avenue pretending that I knew what direction *Eva* would be. I rounded the bend and I looked to the left at a condominium building that had a sign that read, "The Crescent Park Waikiki." There was a listing that I had circled for a rental in this building. I would make a mental note to return here after visiting the bank.

I had to take a short detour from my intended route; earlier this morning the famous Waikiki Biltmore had been carefully imploded a few blocks away from the bank. The destruction of the hotel was necessary for the developer Charles Hemmeter to develop two 40-story towers which were to become the Hemmeter Center and the Waikiki Hyatt Regency hotel.

Bank of Hawaii was located directly across from the beach in the middle of Waikiki on Kalakaua Avenue. There were so many unexpected sights on Kalakaua Avenue that I passed along the way to the Bank. The Waikiki Theatre designed in an art deco style and St. Augustine by the Sea Catholic Church, they were amongst several hotels of differing architecture. The Waikiki Circle Hotel, the vibrant pink Royal Hawaiian Hotel sitting next to the bright white Moana Surfrider Hotel were the beautiful stars of the beach. They were inviting their guests to bask in the sunshine, swim in the sea, and drink in the warm air. I was already envious of the families that could stay right on the beach in these beautiful hotels. "How blessed are they!"

I walked into the lobby of the Bank of Hawaii and I felt like I was a fish that had just jumped out of the water from the ocean across the street. Casual *Aloha* wear was worn by all who worked at the bank, and the majority of the customers as well. The bright Hawaiian shirts reflected the bright and cheery disposition of the staff. It was clearly a uniform, all of the different prints on the shirts had the words Bank of Hawaii mingled with floral scenes and a variety of tapa designs. The bank concierge looked up from her desk and she said, "*Aloha*, how may I help you?"

That beautiful word *Aloha* floated off her lips and landed close to my heart. It would not be long before I would not just learn the meaning of the word, I would learn that *Aloha* is a value, one of unconditional love. *Aloha* is the outpouring and receiving of the spirit of kindness. It is a state of mind that anyone can achieve, native Hawaiian or not. Encapsulated in the word is an implication of hello, goodbye, and I love you. I knew that word would bless my life here in Hawaii.

I said, "I am looking for the HR department to apply for a job that is advertised for a Teller at the Airport branch."

"Follow me, I will take you to Leilani who is in charge of new applicants."

I followed her to the offices that were located behind the teller cages. An elderly woman dressed in a beautiful muumuu with a Kukui nut lei circling her neck greeted me.

"Please fill out our application for employment," she said. "When you have it completed, return it to me along with any forms of reference that you may have."

I had an immediate sense of a loss of action, the first few lines were for Name, Address, and Telephone number. I have at least an answer for one of those requests—Name. I finished the application as best as I could. I handed it back to the woman who had gone back to her desk.

"Would you please be so kind to take a photocopy of my letter of recommendation?" When she returned, she began to read my responses and she asked, "Would you please provide your address and telephone number?"

"I am sorry I just arrived from the mainland yesterday and I will be acquiring a permanent address hopefully later today. A telephone number will be several weeks away after I have moved into my new place of residence. I am presently staying at the Waikiki Grand Hotel in room 707. Please feel free to call there should that become necessary."

"That will not be a problem, I will forward your application to the Airport Branch manager today. They are looking to fill the position as soon as possible. Please give Mr. Ninomoto at the Airport branch office a call tomorrow afternoon."

"Thank you very much, I appreciate the opportunity to apply for this position. I am certain that I could be an asset to your bank, I am available to begin immediately."

"Oh by the way," she said, "please wear a Hawaiian business casual shirt with no tie should you be granted an interview. Every day at the Bank of Hawaii is *Aloha* Friday. We encourage one another to have days filled with beauty, and that all of our moments be happy ones. *Aloha* wear encourages a happiness in providing customer service. We ask others to put their trust in our strengths."

I took careful notice of the men on staff and their attire. I would hope to have my *Aloha* Friday shirt by the end of the day. The magic of *Aloha* had clearly found one willing suspect in me. I felt like I had an invisible Poll Parrot on my shoulder. He was secretly guiding me forward to the next task that was awaiting.

On the way back to the hotel, I stopped by the condo that had a listing that I circled for rent. The real estate executive who was representing the condo at Crescent Park Waikiki at Kuhio Avenue was walking out of the elevator as I arrived. She asked, "Can I help you find someone?"

"I am responding to an ad for a rental that was listed in the newspaper."

She said, "I am the listing agent for that property. This listing is a temporary listing for a brief three-month sublet. My client is in the Orient and he will be returning in September. The unit is fully furnished and no additional furnishing can be moved into the unit."

"That is perfect!"

She responded in a fashion that said let's hurry and get this over with.

"Okay let's have a look, I will take you to the tenth floor to unit number 1021."

When the door was opened, I felt like I was looking at a glossy magazine cover. The views from the wrap-around *lanais* were unimpeded vistas of the zoo, the mountains to the north, and out to the ocean rolling into the shores of Diamond Head.

"Whats is the rental fee?" I asked.

She replied in detail, speaking as if it were a recording. "The rental is $750 per month and there is a $300 refundable cleaning deposit. I have two other interested parties coming by later today."

"Can I give you the deposit right now?" I asked. "Could we move in tomorrow and pay the rental fee then?"

She replied quickly. "I would normally wait until references were verified, however I am very busy today, I have three other appointments that I need to attend to today for long-term rentals. I don't see any reason not to accept your offer."

I took out three $100 bills from my wallet and that sealed the deal. She responded, "Please bring your telephone number with you tomorrow, along with the first month's rent. Let's meet here at 10 am sharp. You won't have to bother with putting the utilities in your name, they are being covered by the owner."

I wasn't sure if it was me or the Parrot that had the idea that perhaps I could use the telephone number of Paul's sister who I had yet to meet. Now that I had an address, I could potentially be able to complete the blank lines on my application at the bank and also provide a telephone contact for the real estate agent. I thought to myself, perhaps things are easier in paradise.

On Wednesday afternoon, I made a call from the pay telephone in the hotel lobby to Mr. Ninomoto at the Bank of Hawaii. He said that he had reviewed my application and my letter of reference. He asked if I could come to his branch Thursday morning at 8 am for an interview. I gladly accepted his invitation, and made a mental note to go shopping for my new Hawaiian business attire *Aloha* shirt. I stopped by a bus stop on my way to the Liberty House Department store to obtain a copy of the bus schedules from a bus driver who was sitting idle. He told me that there was a direct bus to the airport on Ala Wai street several times a day. Perfect! Now onto searching for the *Aloha* attire. I was fortunate to have a sales associate approach me.

"Can I be of assistance, are you looking for *Aloha* wear?"

"Yes I am looking for an appropriate *Aloha* business outfit to wear to an interview at the Bank of Hawaii tomorrow morning."

He replied, "Bank of Hawaii has their own *Aloha* shirts that are produced by one of our suppliers. I will show you similar shirts that you could purchase that would not have the Bank of Hawaii logo on the shirt. We can match that with a pair of light cotton trousers."

As he selected several shirt and pants combinations, I tried not to show that I was looking closely at the prices. I was going to have faith that this investment in my new *Aloha* attire will pay off.

"*Aloha,* thank you for your help. I feel confident that this is exactly the outfit that I will need to secure my new job in the islands."

"*Mahalo a nui loa,*" he replied.

I made a mental note of his response. I would add it to the other new words I would need translation for that I had written down in the past couple of days.

Chapter Four

"HO' OMAKA HOU 'ANA"
new beginnings

Looking closely at the bus schedule, I determined that I needed approximately one hour to get to the airport. I decided to take the safe route and get there an hour early. The ride to the airport was like being on a guided tour. The bus driver was colorful and he announced a variety of stops along the way; Fort DeRussy, AlaMoana, and *Aloha* Tower. When we were close to the Dole Pineapple refinery, there was a blending of the smell of pineapple and fuel oil. The pungent smell was bittersweet and I was not in favor of the aroma. Bus #20 arrived at the Honolulu airport departure terminal fifty minutes after leaving Waikiki. I walked around for a short time before locating the Bank of Hawaii. The bank was located inside the airport on the international arrivals level. There was bit of oddity being back in the lobby of the airport only few days after my arrival. As I was descending on the escalator to the bank level, I looked to the left at the sign above the offices of Deak Perera, Foreign Currency Exchange. Somehow I felt some familiar sight connection to this sign, as if it was a deja vu moment.

At eight o'clock sharp, I was the first one through the door as it was unlocked by the bank manager. I took a stab at hopefully addressing the right person.

"Good Morning Mr. Minomoto, I am Chet Gritzmacher, thank you for the opportunity to meet with you today."

He seemed to be taken back a bit with my forward greeting.

"I am happy that you have come and meet with us at such short notice."

"No problem! I am excited to have this opportunity to possibly join your banking team."

The interview went extremely well. Mr. Minomoto was impressed with my letter of recommendation from the bank in Utah. There were no issues with the length of or lack thereof with my college education. He left for a few minutes and returned with the support services manger.

"*Aloha*, welcome to the Bank of Hawaii. I am Leticia Babalindo. On behalf of Mr. Minomoto and the Bank of Hawaii, we would like to offer you a position as a front line teller. Would you be willing to accept this offer, and when would you be available to begin?"

I stumbled with my response, "*Mahalo*, I would be happy to join your staff. I will be available to begin on Monday morning."

"That's great, if it is okay I would like to take this opportunity to introduce you to the staff. Everyone is here this morning for a staff meeting and it will only take a few minutes of your time."

"Thank you, I can stay as long as you would like."

❀ ❀ ❀ ❀ ❀

Bus #22 was just arriving at the bus stop as I exited the bank. Strangely enough, the bus driver remembered me.

"Welcome back *haole*," he blurted out.

The bus was mostly full. I heard many languages being spoken as I walked to the back of the bus. There was a handful of tourists with all of their bags stacked on their laps. When the bus arrived at the bus stop "Hotel Street" the bus driver sounded like he was announcing to the newly arrived tourists that was the stop for Hotels. I watch them gather their bags, leave the bus, and look strangely at their surroundings from the sidewalk where they were now standing as the bus pulled away. "Hotel Street" was the location of what is carefully referred to as the red light district. The tourists thought that they had arrived at the location of their hotels on "Hotel Street" in Waikiki. Clearly, the bus driver was not sharing his *Aloha* spirit with these *Malahinis'* (newcomers to the islands).

I returned to the Waikiki Grand Hotel late in the afternoon. My roommates had just returned from their 10 am to 2 pm beach time. They looked like a fresh catch of slithery red lobsters all covered in baby oil.

I said, "I have so many things to tell you about. How about we celebrate our first happy hour in Hawaii at Tiki lounge piano bar that is around the corner on Kalakaua Avenue?"

"Sounds great," they said in unison. "Let's do that."

❀ ❀ ❀ ❀ ❀

I waited on the *lanai* for everyone to shower and dress for their evening happy hour adventure. I sat gazing at the unbelievable sites in front of my eyes. Diamond Head was glistening from a fresh dousing of pineapple rains. The deep blue of the Pacific Ocean made a lei around the base of the Volcano encompassing its border as in homage to the spirits. I was completely engulfed in the images and I had my first experience of what I would describe as a sense that there was no temperature. It was not hot, it was not cold, it was perfect to say the least. I was ready to experience my first Hawaiian cocktail as a man of legal drinking age.

We entered the Piano bar, whose sign on the street advertising the daily happy hour attracted us. We sat at the front of the bar that had the beach as its picture window. The glossy black baby grand piano was set at an angle in the rear, nestled close to the narrow service bar. We were very early for the drinking crowd and we wanted to make use of the two-for-one specials that were advertised on the menu cover. Happy hour would be from 4 pm until 6 pm, and the specialty drink of the day was a red wine spritzer. That in itself seemed a bit strange for a first timer in the bar. I was expecting some exotic fruity drink with lots of pineapple sitting on the rim and trimmed with an umbrella. I looked at the prices and determined that those were the more expensive drinks and they would not be offered as a two-for-one item.

"*Aloha* and welcome to the Tiki Lounge what may I bring you from the bar?"

"Red Wine Spritzer," I said.

Jackie requested, "Kaluha and Cream."

Paul, "a Rum and Coke."

Lastly, Shiela said, "Bring me the strongest exotic Hawaiian Drink you have, Oh and lots of fruit."

Paul said, "Chet I cannot believe you are ordering red wine in Hawaii, this is not California. In fact, I am doubtful that they even produce any type of wine here."

I replied, "Do they produce any type of alcohol here, perhaps something made from fermented pineapple?"

"I have spent most of my first month's living expenses in just one day so I ordered the least expensive drink. This is why I wanted us all to be together here tonight so I can explain the events of the past couple of days."

Paul said, "Did you get robbed while you went walking through the Waikiki jungle?"

"No," I said, "it is just the opposite, I've been given so many wonderful gifts via the *Aloha* spirit. While you were all bathing in the sun, I was out arranging our lives. I hope you will understand how this all just fell into place in a very short amount of time."

I went on to tell them about the new apartment that we would be moving into the next day. Jackie's jaw seemed to drop a bit, and she said, "Did you really rent an apartment without any of us having a chance to look at it?"

Shiela came to my rescue. "It sounds like Chet has saved us from taking away any of our daily beach time. Where is this apartment located anyway?"

I described the new apartment and I told them that we could walk by it on our way home. After all, the Condominium tower was only three buildings away from our hotel.

Paul said, "Is this something that we can afford?"

Yes, I paid the $300 deposit and the rent will only be $185 each per month. We won't have to sign a lease as this is only a temporary three-month rental. When you see this place tomorrow, you will be in awe of how perfect the space is. On top of all of that, I have a job that starts on Monday, so I will be able to start saving some money for when we have to sign a lease in a few months in our permanent location."

Paul seemed stunned. "You have a job? Where? How?"

"I start my job on Monday at the Bank of Hawaii, airport branch. Oh and by the way Paul, do you think that I could use your sister Diane's telephone number? I need to provide a telephone number to the landlord and also to the bank."

He said, "Why don't you come with us to the beach tomorrow? We are meeting Diane and Glen at King's beach at 10 am."

"That is perfect, I look forward to meeting them and also to have my first full day at the beach. I think I deserve that."

✻ ✻ ✻ ✻ ✻

I woke up early in anticipation of having a beautiful beach day. I slipped out of the room and I went down to the lobby for coffee. I started walking to the beach and I looked into the windows of the cafe next door. I decided that I would treat myself to an early morning breakfast. The breakfast special of Portuguese sausage, eggs, and papaya with Kona coffee sounded perfect. Looking out toward the beach and the cloud cover, I was hopeful that the skies would clear by the time we were there lying on the sand.

When we arrived at the beach, Diane and her partner Glen had already claimed their space and they had a perimeter next to them saved for us. When they stood up to greet us, I was hoping that it was not so obvious that I was wide-eyed seeing these two beautiful people. Diane had very long silky brown hair, a beautiful body, and wore a gossamer bikini. Glen also had long hair, and incredible moustache and a body that should be on the cover of a suntan lotion ad. Wow!

The cloud cover did not diminish the heat of the day and it was very comfortable lying on the sand with a light trade wind blowing over our bodies. A cloudy day at the beach was still a day at the beach, and it was a beautiful thing. My first swim in the ocean felt like a warm baptism welcoming me into the fold of the islands. We had our fruit punch from the small snack stand that offered not only drinks but also an assortment of plate lunches. All the entrees included the local staple of macaroni salad, white rice, and a choice of either ribs or chicken.

Diane wrote down her telephone number for me and she said that I was welcome to use it for reference. I thanked her and I wrote my name and address on a napkin and gave it to her in case someone called asking for me, she would at least know my name. We stayed for the full designated beach time, 10 am until 2 pm. Diane and Glen had a beautiful Hawaiian tan; Jackie, Paul and Shiela looked like they had been rubbed in butter. I figured that since it was a cloudy day that I didn't have to bother with any Coppertone lotion. New friends, the sand, the sea, and Hawaii had made this day unforgettable.

As the early evening progressed, the clouds floated out of the skies and they no longer carried rain or ushered in a storm, but were only there to add color to my sunset sky. This was the first time that I had the experience of seeing the sun set into the ocean. I watched as the sun gave its last fiery kiss to the night.

I was not ready for my day at the beach to end. I walked along the beach fronts of the hotels that dotted the shoreline of Waikiki. The elegant Royal Hawaiian Hotel mimicked the pink color of the sunset in all its glory. As I got closer, I could hear the beautiful melodic voices of entertainers who seemed to be calling out to the sea. I suddenly felt cold, yet it was at least 75 degrees. I figured it was just my emotions giving me imaginary chicken skin, as the locals would say, or goose bumps to *haoles*. I continued on down the beach to another beach front location and I heard the emcee welcome to the stage the international star Mr. John Rowles. I sat down and I was immediately in awe that I was experiencing this concert on the beach for free. He began his repertoire with a song that spoke of Cheryl Moana Marie, a love song of her waiting to be safely in his arms. I so wanted to be safely in the arms of someone who was there waiting for me.

I started to feel chilly again and I decided that I should begin to go back to the hotel, my shirt and shorts were no longer keeping me comfortable. I could feel that something not right was happening with my face. I put my hands on my face and I felt blisters on most of all of the surfaces available. I did not think for a second that perhaps I had a sunburn. How could that be? There was no sun today, only clouds? When I returned to the hotel room, my roommates were on the *lanai* sipping wine. I opened the door to the *lanai* and stepped out to join them.

"Oh my hell Chet! What has happened to your face?" said Jackie.

"I'm not sure but I am feeling chilled and my face is very uncomfortable."

"Come with me and we will put some cool cloths on your face."

When I looked in the mirror in the bathroom, I could not believe the image coming back at me. I have seen sun burns but never to this extent. Paul called his sister and she and Glen drove over to give us some assistance on how to treat my face. When they came into the room they simply said, "You are coming with us we are going to the doctor now." We drove to the Waikiki free clinic that was on Kuhio Avenue. The clinic was mostly used for STD checks and for emergency medical needs for those in the Waikiki jungle. When I walked in, I expected the nurse to look at me in horror. Calmly she said,

"*Haole* boy don't you know that you need to protect your precious pale skin from the sun? It appears to me that you perhaps have second-degree burns. The nurse practitioner will see you shortly."

"Thank you I appreciate your willingness to see me this evening," I said.

The nurse practitioner basically gave me the same scolding as the nurse. He explained how seriously damaging the sun can be. He sent me home with a heavy white salve that I was to apply in-between cold compresses. He gave me a bottle with a ten-day supply of antibiotics. On the bottle in large words, NO ALCOHOL, damn, I had just enjoyed my first day of adult drinking in the islands, a short-lived enjoyment of liquid libation. That would be okay, hopefully in ten days I would have enough money to buy one of those Happy Hawaiian drinks that Elvis would order, like a Blue Hawaiian.

We had left our slippers outside the clinic next to a sign that said:

Mahalo for removing your slippers
(But no take mo'bettah ones when you leave)

Our slippers were there waiting for us amongst many that mostly looked alike. I had to read the second line on the sign twice to understand the message written in pidgin.

Chapter Five
"OIHANA MAIKAI"
great work

Monday morning came with me having only a couple of days to heal my face and I was off to my first day of work. I was determined that nothing could keep me from showing up for my first day. I felt courageous for just showing up and letting myself be seen. I knew that I could get to the bank by bus but only by hard work and a risk of not quite knowing what I was doing, would I discover myself in this new position. I was proud to have the appropriate clothing to wear, and yet the face that I looked at in the mirror was a horrible sight. There were still a few raised blisters and mostly dried blobs of yellow liquid that continued to ooze out of the wounds. I am not sure if my embarrassment was greater than the horrors of the sight of my face.

Mr. Minomoto greeted me at the door, and said almost the exact words as the nurse.

"*Haole* boy, don't you know the dangers of the sun?"

"I certainly do now, I am very sorry for my appearance."

"That is not a problem," he said. "You will actually not be on the teller line for a few days. We have you enrolled in a training program that is being held at the main branch downtown on Bishop Street. You will be inside with a few others and by the time you return I am sure your wounds will be better. Please take care of yourself and see a doctor to avoid complications."

"Thank you for that, I have seen a nurse practitioner and I've been using what has been prescribed for me. I am certain that I won't be lounging in the sun anytime soon. I have definitely learned my lesson."

I boarded the bus from the airport taking me back to downtown. As I exited the bus, I looked at the various buildings, searching for the Bank of Hawaii sign. On the corner of Bishop Street and King Street there was fountain that was shaped like a volcano, made out of brilliant red bricks. Behind the fountain was sign on a building that I had seen earlier at the airport, "Deak Perera Foreign Exchange." The offices were behind two stories of slightly tinted glass. I could see a very large DP made out of silver that was displayed in the middle of a circle of dark blue velvet. How exotic and titillating the images appeared to me, but for no known reason.

❀ ❀ ❀ ❀ ❀

Things went forward in a seamless fashion. We moved into the condo on Kuhio Street, I started a new job, and my roommates continued to enjoy the daily 10 am until 2 pm beach lounging. I was thankful that I could join them on the beach at least on the weekends. I had discovered sunblock and a hat and I was happy to at least have brown legs.

Three months into our adventure, Shiela started having serious bouts of nausea, fainting at the beach, and she looked pale underneath her great suntan. I suggested that I introduce her to the Waikiki free clinic that I had gone to for my sunburn. We went together and when she came out of the nurse practitioners office, streams of tears were flowing down her cheeks. She said that she wanted to wait until we were home with Jackie and Paul to talk to all of us together.

"I am in my third month of pregnancy," she said. "I had allowed myself a parting night of passion and intimacy with my ex-boyfriend just before were left for Hawaii. What a fool I am! I am going to call my father tomorrow and I am going to ask him to buy me an airline ticket back home. I am devastated, but I am left with no other choices."

We all choked on our responses to Sheila. Surely this can't be the beginning of a slow train back to where we all came from. I was not going to even think that could be an option for me. The following day, Sheila told us that she would be leaving for home on Sunday.

※ ※ ※ ※ ※

With the weekend fast approaching, we decided to make the best of our short time together. We rented a car, if you could call it that. It was a 1974 Volkswagen thing. It was slow, flimsy, and unsafe with no safety equipment whatsoever. It had no top—but why would we care? It had four doors and four seats. The flooring was wood that allowed any sand that you would bring in with you to drop through. The windshield could fold down so you were clearly floating along with the breezes directly on your face. The windows on the doors did not go up or down; you would simply just remove the doors and set them aside behind the seats. The sound that we made coming down the road was like a lawnmower on wheels, and we were going at the same speed. Off we went, temporary tourists for the weekend. We had no map and we thought, how could we get lost on an island? First stop, Hanauma bay. We had not planned on going swimming, however everything that you wear in Hawaii can be used for swimming. We put our toes in the sand and we swam with beautiful brightly colored fish, they were a kaleidoscope of species that were showing off their beauty. This is why we were here.

We bought one-way tickets
We took a break and we packed a bag
We went swimming in the sea
We had made new friends
We had fallen in love with Hawaii
We discovered what matters
We had a great time
We will never look back.

We jumped back in the Wild Thing with the windshield down, and the doors off. We quickly dried ourselves and we followed the shoreline to our next adventure. Kaneohe Bay was glistening and the calm water was calling out to the views of the Chinaman's Hat, which-resembled the shape of a Chinese peasant's head-covering. Onwards we went as the day was quickly slipping by. We continued northward, reaching Sunset Beach and the Banzai Pipeline. There were cars lined along each side of the road for miles. The waves were of historic proportions and everyone wanted to see them and watch the brave surfers attempt to ride the Pipeline. We stopped further up the road and followed the roar of the waves back to the sea. We sat down on the beach in awe of the spectacle in front of us. The mountains of waves were curling 20 feet in the air and creating a tube that the surfers would enter and attempt to use as their highway to exit on the other end. The Banzai Pipeline is one of the biggest and heaviest waves on the planet. The wave itself only lasts about seven seconds.

We had to pull ourselves away from the beach to continue on our journey. The afternoon sun was heading westward and we wanted to cover as much of the island as we could. We followed the signs that directed us to Honolulu.

Pineapples and sugarcane were growing on both sides of the highway as far as we could see. The Dole Pineapple plantation lured us into its parking lot. We were happy to have stopped for facilities and of course for some freshly made pineapple ice cream. Simply an island delicacy. I asked one of the clerks for help with directions back to Waikiki. She told us to follow the road we were on and watch for signs for the *Pali* Highway. We took a small detour to the *Pali* Lookout. It was easy to visualize the site of the Battle of *Nuuanu* where King Kamehameha had won the battle, forcing hundreds of soldiers over *Pali*'s sheer cliffs. The views of Kaneohe Bay and Oahu's lush windward coast are breathtaking as you feel the wind push against you and you hear it whistle through the mountains behind you.

As we slowly made our way down the *Pali*, the windward rains followed us downward towards Waikiki. We were all so soaked with the wonder of the day that we did not even notice that were also soaked with the heavy downpour of the refreshing rains. We saw the bright lights and tall buildings ahead, and we knew that we were back to where the day had began.

We quickly showered so that we could make it to the beach before the last light flickered out into the sea. We walked along the beach to a giant Banyan tree next to the shore. A plaque stated that the tree had began its life in paradise being planted in 1904. It was a Ficus Benghalensis Indian Banyan. The tree was over 75 feet high and 150 feet across. There is much to learn from a Banyan tree, the value of stillness, to live life at your own pace, and to discover your wisdom within. The gales of silence could not uproot me now. I had begun to grow banyan roots in my heart. We gathered around the tree and asked a bystander to take a photo of us. We formed a small circle facing one another and agreed that on this day, Saturday August 17, we would meet again here ten years later in 1984. If tears had a sound, we would be listening to small rivers gliding down our faces. The Hawaiians were whispering in our ears *"A hui hou kakou"*— until we meet again my friends...

❊ ❊ ❊ ❊ ❊

We were now left with a housing dilemma—where to move next? My roommates, who I had begun to love dearly, were still beach rats. There were no jobs in sight for either Paul or Jackie. I decided to do what I had done so far, keep moving forward. I immediately began my search for housing that I could afford to share but only on my income. I had circled several listings that I would begin to call on. I walked to the Star Market at Prince Kuhio square to use the pay telephone. I was immediately turned away by the first five phone calls. The deposits were almost as much as my monthly income. The last call was again for a sublet of an efficiency apartment that was owned by a Japanese firm. They could give us another three months in Paradise without a lease. The owner had several units that he used for Japanese business men who came to work in the islands. The person who had been living there had gone back to Japan for three months to help with the recent birth of his wife's twins.

The agent said, "I will give you a call back tomorrow after I speak with the owner."

I quickly responded, "I am just a few blocks away, can I possibly meet you there today."

She replied, "I was just about to leave Waikiki for my home in *Kalihi*, can you be here in 15 minutes?"

I began to walk to meet her and realized that I had passed by the building that she was going to show me every day going to the bus stop. This was a good thing as this meant that I would not have to change my early morning schedule. Again, the luck of *Aloha* was on my side.

"Yes," she said, "I am willing to hold the unit for you to move in on the 1st day of the month."

The unit was tiny in comparison to our condo. This was an efficiency studio unit. It had a small kitchen, bathroom, a double futon sofa, and a very small *lanai*. The rent was half of what we were currently paying. We would just have to make do.

Chapter Six

"MALAMA NE'E I MAU"
keep moving forward

Paul had shipped his Volkswagen Beetle from the mainland and it arrived two days before we needed to move. I contacted the rental agent concerning a parking stall. Parking was at a premium in Waikiki. Yes there would be a stall for his car, but it would be an additional $100 per month. Three people living on one income had suddenly reached a critical mass. We went over to the new apartment together to receive keys from the agent.

"Hello there, I was only expecting to see you, Chet?"

"Let me introduce you to Jackie and Paul, they will be sharing the apartment with me. I figured that we can make it work for the short three months that we will be here."

"I'm sorry," she said, "I am going to have to speak to the owner. There is a limit of two occupants per unit."

I quickly replied, "We are more than happy to pay a bit more for the space for having three of us here."

Paul spoke up, "Actually we will have very little time here together. Jackie and I will begin our new jobs this weekend and I will be working a night shift and Jackie is working a swing shift. Chet works days so we will hardly overlap our time here."

I tried hard not to stare Paul down with the surprise news of them supposedly having jobs.

The agent replied, "Ok perhaps that won't be a problem after all. I will need $300 for the parking stall. The owner is requesting the payment in full for the three months that you will be here."

"That is fine," said Paul. "I can give you cash for that now."

That whole process with the agent took about 15 minutes time.

"Chet what were you thinking, where are we all supposed to sleep?" said Jackie.

"Don't worry," said Paul. "My sister Diane told me today about a warehouse that has all of the old beds from the Biltmore hotel that they tore down when we first arrived. I went there today with Diane and I will be able to put a couple of single mattresses on top of my car. I figured that I can cover them in fabric and we can use them stacked on top of each other as a futon during the day and separate them to sleep on at night. I am actually quite handy at that kind of thing. Chet I am sorry that you had to learn of our new jobs like you did. We actually received our job offer letters today in Diane's mail. We took them over to the Hilton Hawaiian Village and we signed their letter of acceptance, we will start there on September 8th. We will be shadowing existing staff members for training for a week."

That's just great I thought, I will be turning 21 on September 8th and the only two people I know on the island will be working. So be it, I will treat myself to one of the cocktail shows on the beach and celebrate with everyone in the room.

"Congratulations to you both," I said. "I would love to take you out for a celebratory drink but I paid for the first and last month's rent and I am bone dry until my paycheck in 10 days."

"I think we must all be in the same boat," said Paul. "I spent the last of my cash on my car registration and now on the parking stall. I won't even be able to fill it with gas until I get paid."

Jackie said, "This all seems a bit crazy. I had to pay for a visit to Straub clinic. I fainted at the beach yesterday and a nice man took me to the clinic. It was determined that I was dehydrated and low in calcium. I was given an injection and they wanted payment in full since I did not have insurance."

"I said well there is some good news, we have 5 lbs of ginger snaps and plenty of water, that should last us until next week. Hopefully they will feed you both at work. I always have some international delicacy provided by one of my coworkers and I can eat at the airport lunch room, chili and rice $1.25. I certainly won't starve."

❋ ❋ ❋ ❋ ❋

I received a card in the mail from my mom and dad that I was waiting to open on my birthday. I was hopeful that I would receive a few dollars in the card to be able to use on my birthday. I had an idea for a birthday gift for myself. I was noticing that moustaches were very trendy here in the islands. Unfortunately I could not grow any kind of hair on my face. I did however have quite nice hairy legs that looked fairly good now that I had a significant sun tan. I was on a quest to find a moustache. I had seen a store in the Hawaiian shopping center on Kalakaua Avenue that had all sorts of wigs in the window, and one small shelf with moustaches! I decided that I would open my card from my mom and dad on Friday the 7th of September, one day before what I suspect is a milestone birthday for most people. Mine was going to be perfect, after all I am in paradise. I was so excited to open a wonderful birthday card that was signed, "We miss you son, love Chester and Katie." Included were two crisp $20 bills. That seemed like an amazing amount of money to me. I thought it may just be enough for my moustache. I almost ran to the wig store, I wanted to get there prior to their closing time. I was mildly embarrassed and excited at the same time.

"*Aloha* how may we help you?" said the clerk.

"I am wanting to purchase a moustache that will hopefully match my hair. I want a small moustache that looks real and that I can wear for several hours with no problem with it adhering to my upper lip."

She responded, "We have just received a shipment of stache's from China that are well made and significantly less expensive that those from Japan. I'm quite sure that we can find you one that you will be happy with."

"That's great," I said with a cautious excitement.

After trying on several I found the perfect one. It was lighter in color than my hair and I had kind of a Robert Redford look about me with it glued in place along my lip.

"This is perfect, I will take it. Can you show me the proper way to attach it to my lip? And I will need to purchase the adhesive as well. How long will the adhesive last?"

She said, "As long as you don't get it too wet, or if you don't sweat a lot you should be able to wear it for 6 or 8 hours at a time."

I was planning on wearing the moustache every day except for working at the bank. I left the store with my new hairy lip securely attached. I walked along the beach and somehow this new persona that I had seemed a bit sexy. I was glad that Jackie and Paul were out on the town with Diane and Glen. I would have time to take it off before they returned home. For now this was my little secret. Strange that one can purchase a bit of a new identity, and I was happy for that, I liked it. My new moustache was like a bow tie for my face.

On September 8, 1974 I turned twenty one years of age. I reached the age that I could show my ID and be an adult in all the mainland states. I was immediately legal age when I landed in Honolulu, as the age of adulthood in Hawaii is 18. All the same it was a milestone for me. At the age 16 you can drive, and at the age of 21 you can drink. I am actually not overly interested in either one of those privileges. I had the day and evening all to myself. I started off by going to the beach. I had been in Hawaii for over three months and this was the first day I had gone by myself. I had to think about the caution of sweating before I glued on my moustache, but I decided that I was close enough to our apartment if I had to retreat there for a touch up of glue. I found my spot on the edge of what is known as Queen's beach. It is just a bit further down the coast from Waikiki within walking distance from our condo. Queen's beach has shaded areas on the grass and you can also lay out on the exposed sandy beach. The beach hugs the sparkling blue water, calming ocean waves, and sights that are absolutely amazing. It was hard to ignore the fact that there were definitely more men than women or families on the beach, more speedos than bikinis. I was definitely not the speedo type, I was already skating on the edge with a glued on moustache. I put my beach mat closer to the Waikiki side of the beach, yet close enough to have views of a groups of men enjoying the company of each other, and right here out in the open. I was okay to enjoy that view on my 21st birthday. I almost felt invisible with my new moustache on, a new me was beginning to emerge. I was careful to keep myself lathered in sunscreen, I was not going to ruin my evening with a sunburn.

Returning to our apartment, I was happy to see that my room-mates had already left for their orientation to their new jobs. I spruced myself up, applied a fresh bit of glue to my moustache, and attached it to my lip and I thought my day at the beach had given me a fresh glow. I had taken one of the many flyers from the street kiosks that advertised what entertainment was happening in Waikiki. I was interested in a show that was at the Illikai Hotel. *Loyal Garner "Lady of Love"* was performing at 7 pm and 9 pm. There was a two-drink minimum with no cover charge. I was certain that I had enough for the two drinks. I had my best Hawaiian attire on and I would go to the beach for the sunset and then go into the hotel for the cocktail hour show.

I chose a small table that was fairly close to the front of the stage with a nice view looking out over the beach. When the musicians started playing Hawaiian music that would lead into the introduction of *Loyal Garner*, I had chills of joy from the top of my head to the tips of my toes. I had my first Gin and Tonic in front of me and it tasted awful, it would certainly not be hard to nurse two of the cocktails until the performance was over.

Loyal walked into the room and over to the stage. She was dressed in a flowing muumuu with brightly colored fabric, which seemed to mimic the colors of the hibiscus that were in abundance on the island. She had the voice of an angel, beauty and grace flowed on her every word. There is a transcendent quality to Hawaiian music, something very grounded in it that attaches songs to the culture. I was in the presence of my very own Hawaiian celebrity, there was joy in her voice of love. The magic continued to a great crescendo just as Loyal sang *Kanaka WaiWai* (Just A Closer Walk With Thee) and fireworks began to go off in the harbor below. It was all so natural yet it appeared that it must have been orchestrated. Perhaps they were having fireworks in honor of my birthday, I was going to go with that as an explanation. I had turned 21 years of age in Hawaii, what a wonderful place to move forward into adulthood.

❀ ❀ ❀ ❀ ❀

The small apartment building that we lived in provided me with the opportunity to meet several Japanese people that were in a temporary housing situation. I realized that one of the young Japanese women who lived in my building, also rode the same bus as me. I happened to be sitting next to her one day on my day to work, I turned to her and I said, *"Kon'nichiwa"* (how are you).

She looked directly at me with a shy smile and said, *"Watashi wa genkidesu"* (thank you).

I responded, *"Do itashi mashite"* (you are welcome).

A new friendship had begun. She rode the bus daily to go to work at a small Japanese restaurant in downtown Honolulu. She had a limited knowledge of English and I knew a few words of Japanese that I had learned from my coworkers at the bank. *Do itashi mashite* was one of the first phrases that I learned by pronouncing it—"don't touch my moustache." How appropriate was that for me. She told me that she lived two floors above our apartment. I asked if she would like to have tea with me and we could practice sharing our languages with each other. She said that her husband worked seven days a week so any day would work for her. I suggested that we perhaps could meet late on Sunday afternoons.

"O-namae wa nan desu ka?" she asked.

I was proud to respond that I understood, "My name is Chet."

She said, "*Watashi wa Asuka desu.*"

I said, "Nice to meet you Asuka, see you Sunday."

"Yes," she said, "apartment 907, three o'clock."

We shared a glass of tea in her simple apartment, drinking from beautiful fine bone china. I had purchased an English-Japanese translation book to help with our conversation. We plodded through our first meeting and I suggested that we walk around Waikiki and describe what we saw in both languages. We did that for exactly four weeks. In the fifth week of our meeting, I asked Paul if I could borrow his car to take Asuka on a ride around the island. He was fine with that. We had a wonderful day, traveling all around the island describing the sights in Japanese and in English. We enjoyed our joy of friendship and of learning together. We arrived back to our building just as the sun was setting. Asuka asked me up to her apartment for tea. When she opened the door I saw her facial expression drop. Her husband, who I had not met, was sitting on their futon. He spouted a couple of terse Japanese words and I bid her goodby and I left. I was very concerned for her. The next day on the bus Asuka did not sit by me. I chose to move to the seat next to her. She said,

"*Gomen Nasai*" (I am sorry).

I said "*Wakarimashita*" (I understand).

Our friendship ended as soon as it began. I was sad.

Chapter Seven
"E LIKE MA KA MANAO"
as intended

I became someone who walked around dreaming of what the future may have in store for me. I walked through all of the major hotel lobbies dreaming of staying there with my family who I was sure would be coming to see me. I was in awe of the decor in large floral prints in all kinds of fabrics that did not match in the least. It worked in all of its brash splendor to entice the guests to leave it all behind and enter the world of paradise. The hotels figured if they got the lobby right, it would be their favorite spot of their guests to meet, greet, and return.

I started going to the beach that was closer to our apartment than Queen's Beach. I would walk through the lobbies of the hotels that had beach access. As I walked through the Waikiki Outrigger hotel one Sunday morning, I noticed that there was a sign for Deak Perera Foreign Currency Exchange. This was the third time that my eyes were drawn to images of this sign. At the airport when I first arrived, in downtown Honolulu on Bishop Street, and now in Waikiki. The same large DP made out of silver that was displayed in the middle of a circle of dark blue velvet in the downtown office was displayed here. The offices were very tastefully decorated with deep plush brown carpet and white desks. The office hours indicated that they were open seven days a week. I decided to go inside and talk to the two women that were behind the desks. A beautiful Hawaiian woman with long silky black hair stood up to greet me.

"Aloha how can we help you today? My name is Kamuela and I am the manager."

"Hi," I said. "My name is Chet and I have seen your offices at the airport, downtown, and now here. I somehow feel like I am supposed to work here."

"Wow," said Kamuela, "that's amazing! Where are you working now?"

"I am working at the airport branch of the Bank of Hawaii. I am a line teller. I think that I have the potential to further myself in an international company."

Kamuela said, "Well you are in the right place, our company is located in seven countries of the world and in six other States. Let me introduce you to my assistant Patty."

Patty said, "Hi I've been listening to you and Kamuela, and I think that you should come work here with us! In fact you should call our Manager of the Hawaii offices Mr. Manuel VanGelderen. He will be in the office at Bishop Street at 7 am sharp Monday morning. Perhaps you should give him a call and tell him that we have all chatted."

"That's amazing, thank you so much for sharing. I feel perhaps I may see you again, as a coworker!"

I left and went back home to our apartment forgetting that I was supposed to be going to the beach. I decided that I should read up on Deak Perera from the information that Kamuela and Patty gave me. I decided to memorize the information so that when I talked to Mr. VanGelderen on Monday I would appear well informed about their company.

I was so hyped up I could not sleep on Sunday night. I decided to take an earlier bus on Monday. I had planned on getting off the bus in downtown Honolulu near Bishop Street and finding a pay phone. I thought perhaps Mr. VanGelderen would want me to go right over and meet him. I didn't want to seem to pushy so I waited until 7:05 am to make a call to Deak Perera.

"Good morning Deak Perera," said Mr. VanGeldern.

His accent was not one that I had expected.

"Good morning sir, my name is Chet Gritzmacher and I was given your number by Kamuela and Patty in your Waikiki office. I am inquiring sir if you would have time to meet with me to inquire about a possible career with your company?"

"Oh my Gott did they tell you to call me this morning?"

"Yes, they said that you would be in early today and so I thought I would take a chance and say hello. I appreciate you taking a few more moments of your time this morning to talk with me."

"Thank you Chet for calling, unfortunately we do not have any openings right now. I thank you for your enthusiasm and I appreciate all that you told me that you have read about our company."

"Okay thank you, Mr. VanGelderen I hope to have an opportunity to meet you in the future. May I give you my telephone number at the Bank of Hawaii where I work?"

"Yes," he said, "that would be fine. We actually have a good business relationship with the Bank of Hawaii Foreign Exchange Department. Thank you for calling and enjoy your day."

I finished my call just in the right amount of time to get back on to my usual bus that continued on to the airport.

I felt good about my call and I had a strong sense that I had talked with someone that I may have the pleasure of working with in the future. I may have talked with someone who could help shape my professional course in life.

I was on my lunch break at the Bank of Hawaii eating my chili and rice when Mr. Miomoto's secretary came into the employee lounge and said that I had a telephone call. She said that I could take the call in the small conference room for some privacy. I pushed the telephone line that had a flashing light.

"Hello, this is Chet."

"Mr. Gritzmacher, this is Mr VanGelderen at Deak Perera, how soon do you think that you can be here to meet with me?" I felt a surge tingle throughout my body. I could barely respond in an intelligent way. Was I sitting eating my lunch and daydreaming this event? Dreaming is after all a form of planning, is this a prank call?

"I will check with my supervisor and ask her if I could have some personal time off this afternoon. Would it be okay if I arrive be there by three o'clock? We close out our day and balance the teller line at 2 pm. The bus comes every twenty minutes and I should be able to make that happen. If I am unable take the personal time off, I will let you know."

"Thank you, I look forward to meeting you," he said.

"I am sorry, I will be wearing my Bank of Hawaii Aloha shirt, at least you will have a heads up who to look for. I'm excited to meet you and visit your office."

My supervisor at the bank was very understanding of my short request for some time off. I had worked there for three months and I had not taken personal leave. I was happy that Gianni DiMotto had just given me a good haircut over the weekend. My hair had a bit of a blonde highlight from the sun, I had a bit of a tan, and I looked quite healthy. Off I went.

I entered the front doors of Deak Perea and I immediately knew that I should be working there. I was greeted by the office secretary, Rosemary Ambrosi, who said that she was looking for the haole with the Bank of Hawaii shirt. It was a bit strange that she introduced me to the staff that were in front of the office. Gladys Kawelo, Luzviminda Lanneta, Colleen Lee, and Robert C. Meier. Mr. Meier greeted me in German, he recognized my last name being of German descent. I was instantly embarrassed, as my German was not the best. Rosemary said that Mr. VanGelderen was on a conference call and that he would be out shortly.

The chair I was sitting in had deep blue brushed cotton fabric with shiny stainless steel arms. The chair matched the logo that was hanging from the wall with the big "D" in the middle of a stainless steel frame with deep blue fabric backing. All of the desks were stark white, they all had matching chairs to the one that I was sitting in, but they had rollers. Rosemary told me that she was a transplant from Philadelphia. She said that it had taken her at least a year to feel accepted amongst the locals, now she couldn't imagine ever having to go back to the mainland. I said that I felt very fortunate to be in the islands and that I felt very comfortable living here and in my short time here. I too could not imagine having to go back to the mainland as well.

Mr. VanGelderen came out of the conference room and said, "Well hello Chet, I think I would have recognized you even if you were not wearing your Bank of Hawaii Aloha shirt. Your voice matches your looks."

"I hope that is a good thing, I am so pleased to meet you."

He said, "We don't wear uniforms here, we wear more of an informal business attire. We respect the local Hawaiian wear, however we prefer to wear pressed collared shirts.

"An occasional Aloha shirt on Aloha Friday is welcomed."

I thought to myself, this is so interesting, I've been introduced to the staff, I was informed of what to wear, will I be hired today?

Manuel invited me to join him into his office. His passion for his company and for the variety of services that they offer was speaking to a passion that I was looking for. He shared that he had been transferred from New York City to Honolulu. He said as a Dutch Argentinian, it was a culture shock. But now he felt that he was in exactly the right place. His wife, Marcella, was Italian and she was the former Italian Ambassador to Mexico. I had to pinch myself to think that this whole scenario was playing out right in front of me and I was one of the players. He said, "I am impressed with your story and your wanting to be a part of my team, you are hired, when can you start."

I felt that my body had no weight, I was floating on air.

"I am overwhelmed with your blind faith in me, I will not let you down. I will give my two weeks notice tomorrow. I owe that to the Bank for their trust in me and for giving me a job in Hawaii."

Mr. Van Gelderen said, "I like that you have the integrity to give your notice. I am happy that you will join our Hawaiian ohana at Deak Perera. We won't let you down if you do the same for us. Oh and by the way, you should button down one more button closer to your collar on your shirt, this is not the beach."

I smiled, shook his hand, and said, "I will see you in two weeks. Should I join you here at 7 am?"

He said, "Your day begins at 8 am and ends at 6 pm. I would be happy to have you here at 7 am, perhaps we can learn from each other."

I left the office and I felt like that I could not create this dream if I was imagining this was all true. I suddenly remembered the quote by Walt Disney: "All of our dreams can come true, if we have the courage to pursue them."

As I waited for the bus, I realized that I didn't even ask what my wage would be. At this moment in time I was not concerned, I guess a long as I could pay the rent and buy ginger snaps all would be okay.

Heading back to our apartment, I realized that I had not had an opportunity to spend much time with Jackie and Paul. That in itself was actually okay. Perhaps now we could join forces and have incomes combined a bit to be able to afford a different place to live where we could finally sign a lease. I was ready for a permanent residence in Waikiki, Hawaii—I was here to stay. The School song at my hometown High School said the words Forever & Forever in Tooele. I would have to adjust those words a bit, my forever & forever may be changing locations.

❀ ❀ ❀ ❀ ❀

I stopped by the Star Market, bought flowers, a bottle of wine, and some soda. I would be making Wine spritzers at home tonight. I was happy to see that both Jackie and Paul were at home. I said, "I have so much to tell you. The last 24 hours have been something that dreams are made of. I cannot even believe it myself. Let's look for a new home!"

Chapter Eight
"HO'OMAKAUKAU"
get ready

The winds of change, or perhaps the winds of growth were beginning to blow. I was starting a new exciting job, Jackie and Paul were both working at the Hilton Hawaiian Village, and it was that time to search for a more permanent place to live. I would do what had worked out for the best so far—I would go back to Times Market for a newspaper. I took the paper with me on the bus while heading to my first day of work to begin looking at the rental adds. As the bus was heading down Kuhio Avenue, I noticed a building that stood out with its simple artistic architecture. There was a sign at the entrance, "Four Paddle." I wrote the name and address in the margins of the newspaper ads, referencing the corner of Kuhio and Launiu Streets. I was very careful not to let any of the newsprint smudge my new light blue collared shirt that I has starched and pressed. I also wore a pair of light tan cotton pants and a new pair of dress loafers. I thought perhaps this may be the design of island business attire for working at Deak Perera.

Liberty House had a great selection of quality men's clothing, and I carefully chose two outfits that I could mix and match during the week. When the shoe salesman was bringing me the two selections of shoes that I requested to try on, I noticed a smartly dressed Filipino woman trying on what appeared to be hundreds of shoes. I wondered if that was Imelda Marcos. I had empathy for the salesman shuffling the many pairs of shoes to her and back to the storage room. I made a mental note—don't ever be a woman's shoe salesman at Liberty House.

I walked up to the front doors of Deak Perera just as Manuel exited from the parking terrace. He spotted me from the side entrance of the office which was located at the bottom of the escalator. He waved me over to join him to enter the office. We shook hands and he said, "Welcome to Deak Perera, we are excited to have you work with us. I thought we could go over a few things this morning, I have arranged a call for you at 8 am with the Human Resource representative from our New York City office. She will go over compensation, benefits, and other formalities."

"I ask that you greet me the first thing each morning as you arrive, and the last thing that you do each night before leaving. We are a family here and we depend on one another to achieve our tasks. Punctuality and professionalism are a must. Your desk must be kept uncluttered, there should only be work-related items on it. No personal plants, pictures etc. We maintain confidentiality with our clients and we do not discuss our personal lives at length while at work. Don't worry, this may all sound stringent, but you will see that we also have social times to celebrate with one another outside of the office. We serve a very diverse clientele from many countries. In our office, we have employees who belong to various cultures—Japanese, Chinese, Filipino, Swiss, Italian, and I can't leave me and you out. I am Dutch Argentinian born in Buenos Aires. What is your nationality Chet?"

"My father is of German descent and my mother calls herself Austrian, however that is modern-day Croatia. Both of their parents were fluent in their native language."

Manuel asked, "Do you speak German or Slavic?"

"I have a background in German from high school and college classes. I know a few words of Yugoslavian, but mostly how to swear."

Manual chuckled, "It is so common in America that immigrant families conveniently leave their children out of sharing the knowledge of their first-born languages. It is a shame. In my family growing up, we spoke four languages. My wife and I try to keep our conversation fluent by changing languages that we speak at home weekly."

"That is a wonderful thing. I hope someday to work on bettering my language skills and travel to Europe."

"You are definitely in the right place to begin that process."

I could feel a tingling sensation, as if Tinker Bell had just dropped fairy dust on my head. This is truly happening. All I really need is faith, trust, and a bit of pixie dust.

Manuel continued, "We actually do not have an open position for you. I think it best that we train you in all aspects of our business. This will give you a path to further your abilities to be successful and advance within the company."

"I am honored that you have put your faith in me and I will do my best to learn and be a valuable member of the company."

I spent the rest of the day visiting each of the employees at their desks and listening to them describe their duties. The day seemed to end before it even began. I couldn't believe that nine hours had passed.

I addressed Mr. Van Gelderen, "Good night Manuel have a good evening."

"Chet thank you, let me give you a key to the door and a quick overview of the alarm system. You can park your car on the fourth level of the parking garage."

I said, "I do not have a car so that won't be necessary."

He said, "I take the company car home nightly, but it will be available to you anytime to travel between the offices at the airport and in Waikiki if necessary."

"Thank you for a great first day," I said. "I will see you tomorrow, I need to get going to catch my bus."

I had my newspaper in my hand and a couple of sheets of paper from the recycle bin at work. Instead of circling apartments that were for rent, I was busy writing down all of the names of my co-workers that I had met during the day. I wrote down pertinent tasks that I had been assigned but that I had not been trained on. It was all a whirlwind of beautiful sensory overload. My moustache certainly would not have stayed glued on with the permanent smile that I had acquired.

Everyday at work was a new beginning of new information. The currency exchange part of the business was my first task to understand and participate in. Each morning I would collect the teletype from the telex machine with the opening rates for currency that was sent to us from New York City. There is a six-hour time difference between New York and the islands. Any business that we needed to accomplish from our head office needed to take place in the first couple hours of the day. I began coming into the office before 7 am to update our currency rates for our offices prior to our opening at 8 am. I tried hard to have the updated rates on Mr. VanGelderns desk when he arrived. It was not all smooth sailing, I would get a stern reminder to look very closely at where the decimals were placed for each of the currency's exchange rates. One misplaced decimal could cause disastrous financial results. After my first error that was caught by Mr. VanGelderen, I began comparing our rates to the the rates posted on the Wall Street Journal to identify any glaring differences. The buying and selling between our offices and other local banks such as Bank of Hawaii and the First Hawaiian bank was the first order of each day. There always seemed to be an excess or deficit of a particular currency at one of our locations. We would balance that with transactions from the local banks. These transactions were not just done on paper, the actual currencies needed to be counted, double-checked, and delivered. My daily deliveries and pickups from First Hawaiian Bank made me feel like a double agent. The bag, briefcase, or box that I would use would be different each day. This was to ward off the possibility of someone lurking about watching for a trend. I would also take a different route daily, even jumping on the bus for only one stop on occasion. The only exception to this process was going to the post office to ship currencies abroad. There was a very careful packaging of the currency to have it appear as if it was a gift. These packages were mostly being sent from local immigrant workers to their families in the Philippine islands and Japan. I was amazed at the diligence of these workers that would send most of their weekly earnings to their families abroad. The trips to the post office were always made with two staff members.

❊ ❊ ❊ ❊ ❊

In a few weeks I felt that I had a good grasp of the buying and selling of currencies. Every transaction was double-checked by another staff member, thereby ensuring that there was safety in the numbers. There was no exception to that rule.

Mr. VanGelderen called me into his office first thing on a Thursday morning.

He said, "The HMAS Melbourne Aircraft Carrier from Australia has been in the Pacific doing a joint tactical exercise with the US Navy from Pearl Harbor. They will be coming into Pearl Harbor on Saturday for the weekend leave of the sailors. We have been invited to fly out to the Melbourne aboard a Naval helicopter to exchange their currencies. They want to have that opportunity prior to arriving on the weekend to give their sailors more time to explore and have the proper currency to do so. This is short notice I know, but I would like you to go with me, Kamuela, Rosemary, and Christine from our airport branch to Pearl Harbor first thing tomorrow morning. A representative from the Navy will be here today at 1 pm to brief us on the procedures. We will stay on board the Aircraft carrier and return to Pearl Harbor with the sailors. You are not afraid of helicopters and aircraft carriers, are you?"

I said, "I certainly wouldn't know as I have not been aboard either one, but I am definitely up for the challenge. At least we will all speak the same language!"

Promptly at 1 pm, two Royal Australian Navy commissioned officers arrived. Their uniforms were similar to the uniforms of the

US Navy uniforms I had seen on the sailors in the band at the Iolani Palace. Four large gold buttons glimmered on each side of their dark-double-breasted jackets. Their sleeves had two large stripes of gold embroidered about six inches up from their wrists. They had decorative emblems attached at breast level signifying their rank and achieved awards. The officers removed their hats as they entered our offices. The briefing was short but very informative. Rosemary took shorthand of the proceedings. We were to wear long pants, white shirts, and no open toed shoes, only laced shoes without leather soles that would be slick on the deck. We were instructed to wear a zippered jacket as the ride on the helicopter would be a bit chilly. No photography would be allowed, the official Naval Photographer would be along with us, and he would share photos that he would take of the proceedings. Mr VanGelderen went over our process of exchanging the currency and requested that the Naval Purser to be with us at all times when the transactions would be taking place. He also requested that we be allowed to safely store the currencies in the safe on board. The Officers requested that we bring along a small travel bag with our toiletries and a change of clothing to wear on deck as we arrive in Pearl Harbor. Out of respect, they asked that Manuel and I wear a long-sleeved, pressed shirt with dress pants. The women were were requested not to wear a skirt or dress but rather a formal work suit. Our accommodations on board would be in the officers quarters. We would dine with the ships ranking officers for all meals on board.

After they left, Manuel, Kamuela, Rosemary, Christine, and I went into the conference room. We were all like small children looking at all of the gifts under the tree. We were giddy. We shook off the giggles and got down to business. We had many tasks to achieve before Friday morning. We agreed to meet at the office at 7 am to gather everything and double check the lists that Rosemary had provided us with. We would travel together in the company car to Pearl Harbor. We had been given a pass by the Officers and we were asked to bring our identification. I was so glad that I had just received my Hawaiian Driver's License and I also had a photo identification that was provided for me by Deak Perera.

❀ ❀ ❀ ❀ ❀

We arrived at the designated pier just in time to see the Royal Australian helicopter Navy 28 appear on the horizon of the sea and land in front of us. The pilot and second-in -command climbed off and greeted us. After a few safety briefings we were all aboard. Manuel and I were seated behind each other on the open door side of the aircraft. I had anticipated that the door would have been securely closed prior to take off. That was not the case. Thank God for our earphones and the several seat belts that came over each of our shoulders and around our waist were in place. We took off and banked towards Diamond Head. The pilot chose to give us a bit of tourist ride along Waikiki beach before heading out to sea. There was no separation of fear and excitement for me; I was living out a dream that I had never had. As we headed out to sea, the large door was closed and things felt more safe and definitely more calm. The pilot spoke to us through our headphones and said that our estimated arrival time was in 52 minutes. The winds were calm and the temperature at sea was 71 degrees, and we would be cleared for landing at 8:19. When the aircraft carrier came into view she looked like a giant floating runway. There were a few aircraft visible on the flank side of the deck. I could see the circular helicopter pad markings on the front of the carrier. We circled once around the ship and two sailors with bright light sticks guided us to the center of the circle. When the doors were opened and we were invited to step onto the deck, I was instantly aware that there were no fences along the deck. I felt very vulnerable as we were quite close to the edge. I wanted to crawl and not walk in order not to lose my balance. We were escorted across the deck and down into the belly of the carrier. We climbed down from the flight deck, through the hangar deck, and down to the second deck which housed the rooms for the crew to live and work. We were taken to the Officers Staterooms to begin collecting our currencies and other items that we brought onboard to complete the exchanges. No time was wasted in setting up our area that we would use to stage our makeshift exchange table. Vice Admiral Brian Adams introduced himself to us and welcomed us aboard. We shook hands and he in turn introduced us to the Deputy Chief Rear Admiral Christopher Hammond. Admiral Hammond would be with us throughout our stay. Admiral Chris Barrie the purser would also be right by our side.

We began our work quickly. An announcement was made inviting the first seaman to make their way to our area setup for exchange. The invitations were made by rank. We continued for two hours and we had made our way down to the rank of the Lieutenants. Thereafter we were invited to have lunch with the Officers. White linen table cloths covered the tables, china with the Naval insignias were set in place. We were offered several beverages to begin with and a selection of Australian Beers. We all declined alcoholic beverages, we would participate in that at the end of the day. There was a bit more rocking from side to side of the carrier as the day went on. Sitting down increased that sensation. All of a sudden, Christine turned a pale shade of grey and one of the Medical Officers immediately noticed and helped her up and said that he was going to take her to the infirmary. Admiral Hammond asked if we were okay. He said that even the best of sailors has an occasional bout of seasickness. He assured us the Christine would be better in a few hours. The medical officers were well trained in helping with that issue. We finished our brightly presented lunch and Admiral Hammond said that we would resume our exchange duties in one hour. We agreed that would be fine. Within a half hour, Christine returned and she was looking close to her own self. She had been given an injection, some hydration, and warm broth. We could proceed on time.

We exchange a significant amount of money; these seamen were in for fun times in Honolulu. We were invited to the officer's lounge for cocktails at 7 pm. We all chose to stay with sipping a few delicious Australian beers. Dinner was served promptly at 8 pm and we were escorted to our individual sleeping quarters at 9 pm. We were all ready for a rest, it had been and exhilarating yet tiresome day.

At 5 am, we heard the announcement by Chief Rear Admiral Hammond defining the upcoming requirements by the seaman. All hands were to be on deck in dress uniforms at 6 am as we would be entering Pearl Harbor at first sun light. A quiet homage would be announced to honor those that had perished in the attack on Pearl Harbor.

The next morning we quickly dressed and joined the officers for a light breakfast. The formality of this event was enlightening yet sobering at the same time. We joined the crew on deck as we silently entered into the entrance of Pearl Harbor. There was total silence other than the voice of the officer announcing each fallen ship that we passed. There didn't seem to be a dry eye onboard. The severity of the loss of the attack pierced our souls. It seemed inconceivable as we passed the Pearl Harbor National Memorial that what we were seeing sights of destruction that had actually happened. It was a blatant reminder of the privileges that we enjoy and to remember that men died for us to have these privileges today.

We all returned to the company car in silence. We had all been touched and the events of the past couple of days would forever live on with us.

❀ ❀ ❀ ❀ ❀

I was on a tight schedule during the weekend. I had contacted several agents about available rentals in Waikiki. One that had my attention was "Four Paddle" Waikiki. Unit 702. Studio one year lease. Reasonable. I had an appointment for 3 pm. I met the agent at the unit. The unit had unspoiled views of all of Waikiki. I liked that it did not feel like it was too high. Even though it was on the seventh floor, it was just two floors above the pool and recreation area. My immediate thought was this perfect, but I did not want to seem to anxious. The agent said that the owner worked for the Dillingham Land Corporation and he had purchased it as an investment. He was in Saudi Arabia working and he was not expected to be back in Hawaii for at least three years. He did however require a one year lease. There were no furnishings therefore he also did not require a cleaning deposit. The studio was only 460 square feet and it was intended for two occupants. The agent asked if I had work and rental references. I said I did but added that they had all been fairly short. I told her that I was recently employed by an international Company Deak Perera. Her ears perked up as I rolled the name of employer off my tongue. She said, "Oh my heck, my husband is a firefighter and the Chief's wife Kamuela works for Deak. I said, "That's such a coincidence, Kamuela is a coworker of mine and I respect her very much. You can certainly contact her for a reference." The skids seemed to be greased, I was confident that my application to rent the unit would certainly be approved. She said that she would give Kamuela a call and that would be sufficient and she would not require any other references. The unit was mine on the spot. Wow...

I was wondering if I could pull off another surprise at Happy hour with Paul and Jackie. I had already decided that I did not feel bad about making this decision. The lease was in my name and if I had to live alone and pay all the rent, I could barely make it on my new salary and that was okay. I was hopeful that they would join me and not feel slighted that I had yet made another decision for our small group. Since I had the been given the key on the spot from the agent, I decided to adopt a different tactic.

I knew that Paul and Jackie had every other Sunday off. I headed out before they woke up. I left a note on the kitchen table for Paul and Jackie. "Please meet me at 1740 Kuhio Avenue Unit 702 at 6 pm sharp. Perhaps you may want to stay a while... Chet."

I made three trips to the Star Market and I took just a few small essentials to the unit. I bought a beautiful bouquet of Hawaiian flowers and a nice bottle of Champagne. I put them on the kitchen counter top along with some macadamia nuts, papayas, dried shrimp, and dried cuttlefish to be dipped in soy. I had learned to like those items while spending time with Asuka. There were no beds, no futons, no tables, nothing. There were however two chairs on the large *lanai*. We had the two mattresses that Paul had moved to our apartment and that would be the extent of our furniture. That was the least of my worries. I wasn't worried at all, this was all what the land of *Aloha* had intended for me.

I sat quietly on the *lanai* soaking in all of the beauty that was before me. I watched the outside glass elevator go up and down the Sheraton Waikiki. Each time I saw it gliding back up to the top, I thought to myself that the people in that elevator are so brave. I had felt like I had been to the top of the world over the past couple of days. I had not even had an opportunity to tell Jackie and Paul about my adventure with the Royal Australian Navy. I was a bit anxious about telling them that I had just signed a lease on this studio. It was after 6 pm and they had now arrived. I suddenly realized that I they did not have the code to get into the building. I ran downstairs just in time to see them starting to walk away. I opened the door and yelled out to them, *"Aloha* welcome to your new home." That had not been the way that I had anticipated telling them, however somehow it felt exactly like the right way. I decided to take the elevator with them, which took all of the bravery that I had onboard for the day. They were both very silent on the way up. When I opened the door and they walked in, they said in unison, "Are you kidding?"

"No I signed a year lease for this unit just this afternoon at 3 o'clock."

I looked at their faces and I saw the reflection of the sun setting in the beautiful blue ocean that would be there for us to enjoy every evening. What a perfect crescendo ending to the day. How can anyone say no to a sunset.

"Oh and by the way, I stayed overnight aboard the Royal Australian Navy aircraft carrier Melbourne last night. They dropped me off at Pearl Harbor this morning."

Paul said, "Have you been smoking some of the *Paka Lolo* that they are selling on the street?"

"I laughed out loud and said, no I have not! Let's open the Champagne and I will tell you the rest of the story."

Chapter Nine

"ME KE ALOHA PUMEHANA"
with the warmth of my love

There were not many things that happened in my life that I could call routine. I had a new job that was exciting and quite demanding and it brought a new *ohana* into my life. I had a new apartment with no furnishing, I was sleeping on the floor, but I had a *lanai* with a stunning unobstructed view of the ocean and always a sunset.

Thanksgiving was about a month away and I was determined to cook my first meal of celebration and share it with others. With the help of Jackie and Paul, we were able to put together a livable space. We had two mattresses on the bedroom floor, a futon and a small dining table in the living area, and four bar stools. There is only so much that you can put into 400 square feet. We seemed to not want for much. Communication was still difficult without having a telephone. Mr. VanGeldern was concerned that he had no way to contact me after office hours if need be. He offered to reimburse me for the cost of a landline. I jumped on that and it felt good to have that link back in place to be able to contact my family in the mainland. The telephone connection to the United States was actually made with a cable under the sea that went from coast to coast. I swore that I could hear the ocean when calling home. The connection was poor, it was almost impossible to obtain a line to call during holiday periods, a constant busy signal was not unusual.

I began to establish new patterns of living in the islands. I continued to take the same bus to work, I would only have a half an hour to the downtown Honolulu stop. Another *ohana* began to develop with fellow passengers that I would meet daily on the same route. I often sat next to a nice looking local man. He had introduced himself on one of our rides together. His name was Al Martin and he was of Hawaiian Portuguese decent. He was very handsome, had a very positive attitude, and he grew his own moustache. He worked at a salon in Pearl City, which was near the airport. We had great conversations and he found my story to be a bit strange. He particularly loved my story about my purchased moustache and he suggested that I surprise my coworkers and wear it to work some day soon. I said that would not happen but perhaps I would see him in Waikiki one weekend and he would have to look twice to recognize. me. Al made a suggestion that we meet on Sunday for breakfast at Zippys. He was off on that day and he said that he would have some time to show me around a bit. I had not had an opportunity to explore the perimeter of Waikiki, my path was from home to work, and from home to the beach. I was happy to have met a local, a handsome one at that, who would share his time and show me a bit of his life as a local.

We had a fun breakfast and he steered me away from the local special "Loco Moco." He felt the gravy, beef, eggs, and rice were a heart attack waiting to happen. Al said he spent a lot of time in the gym and it was wrong to waste all that time on a bad diet. He asked if I wanted to tag along with him during the day. I was happy to do that and see how the locals live. We went shopping at the Star Market and he pointed out the benefits of fresh broccoli and lemons. We walked back through the Waikiki Jungle on Kuhio Avenue and he suggested that I not walk there alone at night.

He was smiling as he said, "It is well known that they eat *haoles* there at night. You should walk beach side at night and not on the interior streets between the beach and the Ala Wai Canal. Be safe, my friend. I am taking the bus this afternoon to Kaneohe to visit with my *Tutu*, Grandma to you. Would you like to join me?"

I said, "Yes" almost too eagerly. "I would love to go along with you and meet your grandmother."

"Great, let's meet at our regular bus stop at 11:45 and we can take the express bus to Kaneohe."

On the way to Kaneohe, Al told me about his background. His father had come to Hawaii as an officer in the Air Force. He met Al's mother at a local club, they dated for one week, and got married. After only two months of marriage, his father was transferred overseas to Germany. He said that he would send for his wife and take her with him to her homeland in Portugal. He did not send for her, he did not take her to Portugal, he only sent divorce papers to be signed.

We were going to Kaneohe to have lunch with his Portuguese grandmother. We had a short walk into a neighborhood that was a few blocks from the bus stop. I was thrilled to see all of the beautiful yards with a plethora of plants and flowers. We stopped in front of a house that one would look at and say a hoarder lives here. A hoarder in the sense of lots and lots of plants and flowers. There was every kind of container imaginable filled with very happy plants looking like they were ready to be taken to market to sell.

"This is my *Tutu's* house, and as you can see she loves to plant and garden. Each time that I come to visit I take back all that I can carry on the bus. Perhaps she may offer you a few to take back as well."

"That would be amazing. I have nothing growing on our *lanai* and a bit of greenery would be great."

We took off our flip-flops and Al opened the door and called out to his grandmother. She was sitting at a very cluttered dining room table. She slowly stood up to great us and said, "Those bastards across the street are doing it again to me. They are sending me pain in my back. I know they have dolls out and they are thrusting the needles into my back. That will stop soon, I have mine right here and

I will be sending it back to them." She looked at me and said, "*Aloha*, young man, I am happy to see my grandson bring you with him."

"*Aloha*, I am Chet. Al is a new friend of mine and I was so happy that he invited me to visit you. I am pleased to have you welcome me into your home, I am so happy to meet Al's *ohana*. You are quite the gardener and I can't wait to have you introduce me to some of your plants."

"I'm happy to do that," she said. "We will have to be in the back-yard, I can't let the bastards across the street see me today. In fact give me a few minutes to send the pain back to them. Al will you please take Chet to the back yard and I will join you shortly."

We went outside and Al said, "I am sorry I didn't think that you would be introduced to the voodoo dolls on your first visit. You know she is a very well educated woman, she retired as an Adjudicate Judge. I suppose you would not have guessed that."

As I began to respond, she called out to Al to help her bring us tea with lemonade and mint and other herbs. She said that the com-bination of liquid and herbs is used to clear thoughts and open the senses. She took me by the hand and we carefully walked amongst the plants. I asked her the names of a few of the plantlings and pointed out a couple that I told her that I had not seen before. I told her that I thought that they were exotic and beautiful and that she too held that image. She picked up a red ginger plant and said that I should take it to my home to ward off evil and to bring good spirits to me. Along the way, she grabbed a plant that looked like a bloom-ing flowing volcano and a small bird of paradise. I thanked her and said that I would take good care of them. Al had already prepared a bag for me to carry them on the bus; he already had one for himself filled to the brim. She stood and said, "*Vou Nessa*" (I have to run), and she disappeared into the house. Al said that she did not like to say goodbyes and that we could leave by way of the garage.

Al asked, "Were you freaked out by *Tutu* and the voodoo dolls?"

"Not in the least, it added to all of the colorful experiences that I've been having since I moved to Hawaii. Thank you for including me and introducing me to a part of your family and your heritage. I have decided to cook a Thanksgiving dinner next week on Thursday, would you like to join us? I'm not sure of the guest list yet, so far it is me, you and a few others that I perhaps don't know yet."

Al said, "I would love to come, and I would like to bring my specialty Portuguese dish to share 'Vina Dosh.' I will look forward to meeting a few others that I too have yet to know."

Al turned back toward me as he left the bus.

"*Aloha*, my friend."

I held my bag of plants close as I quickly made my way back home to the Four Paddle hoping to be able to share the events of my day with Jackie and Paul and introduce them to our new plant mates.

When I got to the corner of our building, a local boy came over to me and said, "Hey *haole* I see you have plants, want to buy some Kona Gold weed, the best on the island. Only $10 for a small baggie."

"Sure," I said.

He dropped a baggie into the bag that held my other plants. He was gone and I was securely in the elevator on the way to our apartment. I had never thought of an elevator as being secure, but at this time I was alone and not yet arrested and that felt good. I think I may have just done something that may perhaps have been illegal.

Jackie and Paul were in their Hilton Hawaiian Village uniforms and about ready to head off to work. I had put the baggie in my pocket prior to entering the apartment. I took out the plants and they asked where I had bought them. I said that I had just returned from Kaneohe and that they were a gift. I said I would fill them in later. Paul said, "For someone that has no car you sure seem to get around."

I said, "Transportation on the bus is convenient and cheap. I actually don't miss driving anywhere, besides we have your car when we have to bring something large home, I am thankful for that. You guys have a good night at work and I will see you on your day off Tuesday."

I wondered what to do with the marijuana that I bought. I had never smoked it and I didn't have any idea where I was going to keep it in our apartment. As long as the baggie was closed tightly, there was no smell. I ended up putting it in the box that contained my stationary and other mailing items. I wasn't sure about when, where, or how I would smoke it.

❋ ❋ ❋ ❋ ❋

Manuel informed me when I went to work on Monday that an auditor from the New York City office was coming to town on Tuesday. He had arranged a staff meeting for everyone to meet at the Sheraton Waikiki at 6 am so that we could all get acquainted, have breakfast, and then go to our respective offices in time for opening hours. I had wanted to get a haircut sometime soon, so tonight I would try to get one after work. I had noticed that there was a small salon directly across the street from our building. I would go straight there after work and hopefully be in time to get a cut before they closed. I went down a small side alley to the "Gianni D'Amato Hair Hawaii Salon." I walked in and my first thought was that they had forgotten to close and lock the door as no one was in sight.

I said, "Hello are you still open?" A very tanned man with long hair wearing a white gauze shirt and linen pants stepped out of the back and greeted me.

"Is there any chance that I could get a haircut tonight?" He paused for a second and said, "You are in luck, my boyfriend is flying in late tonight from the mainland so I have some extra time."

He seemed so free to share that he had a boyfriend, I almost felt myself flush at his openness. We had casual chit-chat about where I was from, when did I get to the islands, and did I enjoy smoking the local Kona Gold. I tried not to sound naive.

"I have not had an opportunity to smoke any of the local Marijuana, as a matter of fact I have not smoked anything at all."

I did not let him know that I had just bought a baggie.

He told me, "You need to be careful who you buy it from as a lot of it is not the real deal. He said anything that is cheap is just that, cheap and not worth the time. As a matter of fact, I happen to have an extra small bag that I would be happy to sell you. I'll give you a deal since you are now my newest client."

"Thanks, I will take you up on your offer."

He finished cutting my hair and said that he would be right back. He lived above the salon and he went to get the baggie of Kona Gold for me.

I said, "I will need some instruction on how to smoke it."

"*Oh mio dio*," he said, "you are a virgin smoker, are you a virgin in other ways as well?"

I was still sitting in front of the mirror and my face went a bright red, looking very much like my first sun burn.

"I guess you are not Italian, Oh my God you are a virgin!"

I was happy that he did not pursue an answer from me from any of virgin questions. He handed me the baggie that had a very small matchstick sized wrapper inside. He took the wrapper out and pulled out a very thin piece of paper about three inches long. He put a small amount of the marijuana on the middle of the paper he licked the edge and rolled it up.

"There you go, would you care to light up?"

"No thank you," I said. "I have a meeting first thing in the morning and I certainly don't want to have any kind of a hangover."

He said, "I think you will be fine, you will notice that a hangover from alcohol is bad, a pot hangover only lasts a few hours after smoking your joint. Take it slow and you will find something that you will enjoy."

I said, "This may sound a bit crazy, I am having a Thanksgiving dinner next Thursday with several new people that I have met. Would you care to join us?"

"*Mama Mia*, of course! My boyfriend's parents will be in town and they have not met me yet and he thinks it best that we have a separate dinner on Thanksgiving. Count me in..."

I said, "*Mahalo* for the haircut and the Kona Gold. I had a nice time chatting with you and I so appreciate your openness, I look forward to hearing about your adventures here in Hawaii. I live right across the street in the Four Paddle so you won't have far to go. I will stop by and tell you what time we will all be gathering after I figure that part out. *Arrivederci!*"

I went home thinking that I was either brave or crazy inviting strangers over for dinner. I had met Al only a few weeks ago and now Gianni only today. I knew that Jackie and Paul were working on that day so perhaps I could invite Paul's sister Diane and her boyfriend Glen. There seemed to be safety in numbers, and five sounded like the right amount of people. We had four chairs at the dining room table and I could bring in one of the chairs from the *lanai*, there would be enough seating at the table of my first Thanksgiving in Hawaii.

I left for the Sheraton Waikiki with plenty of time to arrive on time for the meeting. A short, somewhat hunched over older Japanese woman was picking up the dead leaves that had fallen from the gigantic rubber tree on the corner next to our building. I had seen her a couple of times before and I assumed the condo association had hired her to maintain the small amount of plantings around our building. I thought that she looked very peaceful and that she enjoyed her gardening tasks. The streets were empty with only a few workers cleaning the walks. The sun had not risen and there was a soft quiet to the waves rolling in to the beach. The sunrise and sunset times in Hawaii do not change much during the year. The sunrise is around 6:30 am and the sunset around 6 pm.

I felt like I knew the Sheraton Waikiki well as I looked directly at it from my *lanai*. I often watched the outdoor elevator ascend and descend to the 32nd floor full of recently arrived tourists. It is a lovely Japanese owned landmark on the beach and being only three years old there was no obvious wear to the building or grounds. The magnificent open air circular two-story lobby was a welcome site to any traveler. Bright deep green and yellow carpet with a large leaf pattern was covering the floors. On top of the carpet were sitting areas of sofas covered in a fabric with brilliantly colored bird of paradise and heliconias. Large bowls hung from the ceiling filled with hanging plants. The lobby was its own sort of fairy land.

I entered into the lobby and I heard Mr. VanGeldern call out to me. "Chet, I knew that you would be here early, I can use your help with setting up. I would like you introduce you to my wife Marcella."

"It is my pleasure to meet you Marcella. You are as lovely as Manuel's description of you, and your dress is beautiful."

"*Graci*," she responded. "Manuel speaks very highly of you; it is a pleasure to meet you as well."

The breakfast meeting was very informative and I felt right at home with my family of coworkers. Manuel invited me to ride with him, Marcella, and Mr. Tobias from New York to go back to the office. I was happy for that and I felt privileged to be in their company. Manuel drove by their home at 250 Ohua Street to retrieve a document that he needed to take to the office. I had not been aware that he and I both lived very close to one another in Waikiki. Instantly, I was planning a holiday cocktail party that would include Marcella and him.

Chapter Ten

"HAU'OLI LA HO'OMAIKA'I"
happy thanksgiving

With Thanksgiving only being a week away I had lots to gather together. I stopped by Paul's sisters house and left and invitation for her and Glen, I wrote down our new telephone number and I asked if she could call to confirm. She called and said that they were happy to come and they would bring a dessert. I was beginning to feel a bit uneasy about my decision to host a meal that I needed to prepare. We had very little furniture, two pans, and barely enough diner ware that I had purchased in Chinatown at a market that sold second-hand items.

I had a very busy week at work with meetings with the directors and the auditor from New York. I was tired when I got off the bus and walked home. I thought for a brief second that I would stop at "Hulas Bar and Lei Stand" for a cocktail. I nixed that idea and decided to have a beer on the *lanai* and relax. I took off my work attire and just put on a pair of shorts. It was always surprising to me that I could be bare chested on the *lanai* at night and not feel chilly. I took a sip of my beer and I thought maybe this would be a good time to try my Kona Gold. I looked at the other *lanais* near me and there were no other people outside. I took out my stationary box and took out the rolled refer from the baggie. I immediately realized that I didn't have any matches. I looked in all of the drawers in the kitchen to no avail. I remembered that Paul had a candle on the bathroom vanity. Luckily, I found a book of matches under the sink. I was set.

I took a couple of puffs from the refer and immediately begin to cough. I thought perhaps I wasn't supposed to inhale so deeply. I took several shallow hits and decided to douse the refer and have the remainder of it another day. I started having some minor lightheadedness. I sat down and looked at the beautiful Waikiki skyline. The ocean gleamed brightly under the light of the full moon, reflections of the hotel lights bounced off the glassy surface of the waves. The Sheraton Waikiki looked gigantic next to the other hotels along the shore. My eyes locked on the brightly lit outdoor elevator. I watched the elevator go up the side of hotel, yet it never seemed to make it to the top. I turned my head to the right and I knew that I had physically moved my head but it took a few seconds for my mind to follow suite and follow. I realized I must be stoned. I wasn't sure if I liked it or not. I grabbed my beer and decided to go inside and rest a bit. I fell asleep on the futon that Jackie used as her bed. I did not wake up when she entered the apartment. She gave me a little shake and said, "Chet are you okay?"

"Yes I am just exhausted, I will see you in the morning."

I went to bed thankful that I had enough sense to put my half smoked marijuana refer back under the stationary in my box. I was certain that the small bit of ashes that I put in one of the plants on the *lanai* would go unnoticed.

I woke up the next morning actually not feeling too bad after experiencing my first smoking of "Kona Gold" *Paka Lolo*. I figured that my parched dry mouth was a result of the combination of the beer and the marijuana, I would make a mental note not to combine the two in the future.

I quickly showered and dressed, I left knowing that I had a lot to purchase for my upcoming dinner. It was quite a chore having to carry all of the items home from the market a bit at a time. Fortunately the market was close by and I could walk back and forth from home and not have to take the bus. The clerk at the Star Market asked me on my second trip if I wanted to take one of the carts home and bring it back. I politely declined her offer.

I had found that having just a couple of shallow puffs on the marijuana helped calm my anxieties at night and I enjoyed having that option if I needed it. Before my guests arrived I did just that. I would keep that pleasure only open to myself.

I had asked everyone to bring what they choose to drink. I purchased two bottles of wine to be served along with our meal, I was as ready as I was going to be.

Al arrived first, he entered and gave me a hug that was both welcome and unwelcome. He said that he lived only two blocks away, he said he had often admired the Four Paddle building. He went out on the *lanai* and he said we need to check out the pool together sometime soon. I was starting to feel uncomfortable about the suggested togetherness, I was not okay with that. Thankfully, Diane and Glen arrived breaking up the bit of ice that I was building around myself. We all grabbed our beverages and we walked out onto the large *lanai*. No entertainment was needed as well all watched the impending sunset. The last of the door knocks occurred and I welcome Gianni into our gathering. Al looked up and instantly approached Gianni with a big hug and said to him, "Who invited you here?" The six degrees of separation was in action. Gianni and Al knew each other socially and Glen had been going to Gianni for hair and beard trims over the past year. I swore to myself that I could not have made this up if I had tried. *Ohana* was in abundance everywhere here in Waikiki.

Dinner came about slowly and everyone pitched in to help with preparation, presentation, and cleanup. We all gathered back out on the *lanai*, Gianni said that he had brought an after-dinner treat. He brought out a baggie of refers and he handed one to each of us. Such a strange occurrence of events. As we puffed away I was so anxious that Jackie and Paul would come home before the event was over, what would they think of me? At the the end of the day, it was just another day in paradise.

❀ ❀ ❀ ❀ ❀

I went to beach in front of the Sheraton Waikiki on Saturday. The beach was very crowded, so I walked further down towards Diamond Head. As I was walking along the beach I was approached a couple of times by someone offering to sell me a ticket to the Party Cruise that night. I took one of the flyers, it looked like fun. The cruise was departing at Sunset from the pier next to *Aloha* Tower. The longer I lay in the sun the more I took in the excitement of the groups of tourists around me. I was going to go. I was going to be amongst those tourists tonight. I figured that tonight was actually a good time to go, I had taken Manuel and Marcella to the airport Friday night and I was to pick them up on Sunday. They were going to the Big Island to visit the Anthurium farm that the company owned and was operated by the Barron and Baroness VanRouge Lewinsky. They were an aristocratic family from Germany that immigrated to Hawaii after the war; they were now working for Deak Perera.

I would have transportation to the Pier at the *Aloha* Tower since I had brought the company car home with me.

I arrived at the Pier and I was surprised at the size of the ship. It was a beautiful white yacht with three levels of outdoor decks and three indoor bars. There were more people than I had wanted to be with, the crowds waiting to board felt a bit claustrophobic. We departed from the Pier and I had my wristband securely attached to my wrist that identified that I had paid for the unlimited drink package. I certainly had not put much thought in that purchase. I had to wait in line for quite a while to get my cocktails. I decided that I would ask for two, and tell them that my traveling partner was sitting down due to the rocking of the ship. I took my two Mai Tai's out on the deck and watched the coast line of Waikiki go by. The waves were a bit stronger than during the day and the ship had quite a bit of movement. I stood in line twice for an additional two Mai Tai's. I felt a bit queasy but not so bad after all of the drinking that I had done. As we were departing down the gangway, I tripped and fell onto the planks. Two very handsome people helped me get up.

They asked, "Are you okay?"

"Yes I must have just tripped."

The woman said, "I think perhaps you may have had one too many?"

"Maybe," I said.

She asked, "How are you going to get home?"

"My car is parked at the *Aloha* Tower parking lot."

"We are also parked there." she replied. "We would like to help you be safe, my husband can drive your car and take you home and I would follow along."

I said, "I will be okay."

She said, "That isn't happening."

I got in to the passenger seat of the Deak Mobile and my newest acquaintance Johnathan was in the driver's seat. He said to me that I was safe with him, that alcohol was not his choice substance for fun. We realized on the way home that he and his wife were staying in a hotel within one block of my home. I suggested that he take one of the on-street parking spots next to his hotel and that I would walk to home from there. I thanked him for driving me home, he handed me the keys and said why don't you come up for a visit and we can get acquainted with each other a bit. He said that they were traveling with a group and I could meet a few of them as well. I went up to the suite of rooms on the 15th floor that his group were occupying. They were all from a successful IT company in the bay area and this was a bonus trip for their contribution to a very successful year. They had the whole floor. Most of the doors were propped open and a variety of music came from each room. We entered his room and I met several of his colleagues. I was just in time to participate in downing shots of Kaluha. That certainly was not the right thing for me to do. After the second shot I had to quickly find a bathroom. I found the toilet just in time and close the door not to embarrass myself too much. When I came out of the door from the toilet room I saw two people hunched over the vanity with small straws in their noses. They were inhaling a line of white powder. One of them looked up at and me and said, "Hey man would you like you could use a line."

"No thank you, but thank you for asking."

The dreaded stomach sickness from way too much alcohol came back with a revenge. I spent longer in the toilet room at this point. The toilet was spinning and I had to hold on. I walked out of the toilet room and I decided that I should lay down for a bit. I found a corner in the open dressing room.

I woke up on Sunday morning with a horrible headache, my hangover was telling my body that I was an idiot. I gathered my senses and realized that I was in a room filled will people sleeping on sofas, beds and the floors. Thank god they were fully dressed and I too hadn't lost a single item of clothing. I sheepishly and quietly walk out of the room, down the elevator and back to my home.

Jackie and Paul were up having coffee, they looked at me and said, "What in the hell happened to you, we were very worried about you?"

"I am sorry I was on a party cruise overnight."

"Now I just need to have a glass of milk and take as rest, I need to pick up Manuel and Marcella this afternoon from the airport."

I put my hand in my pocket and I was happy to have the keys to the company car. I didn't remember much from last night but the fact that I needed sunglasses to open the fridge said it all. Yes I was an idiot, that would not happen to me again. I could not go back and change the beginning, but I could start where I was and change the ending. I had no regrets yet, but I did have lessons that I had learned.

Manuel and Marcella were right on time. I parked and I met them at the gate with two very simple orchid leis. I bid them *Aloha* and gave them their leis, and they both kissed me on my cheek. It felt strange to have that greeting from them, but then again that is how many in the European cultures greet one another. Manuel suggested that I join them for dinner that evening at Arthur's restaurant. I knew of that restaurant from what I had read in a local entertainment magazine. It was known as the celebrity restaurant where the local entertainers would go for dinner following their evening shows at the hotels. I thanked them for the invitation. I told them that I lived right across the street from the restaurant and I would meet them at 8 o'clock sharp. I had a couple of hours to spare, I could quickly walk to Liberty house and buy something appropriate to wear to a nice restaurant. I was fortunate to have saved a few dollars for an emergency like this.

A handsome, yet effeminate man with painted eyebrows helped me pick out an appropriate outfit. He said that he had accompanied a couple of dates to Arthurs, he had good advice regarding what to wear. He was right and it saved me a lot of time trying to guess what I should wear.

The restaurant was quite dark and very formal. Manual and Marcella were sitting in one of the cozy half circled booths that lined the perimeter of the restaurant with a round bar in the center. I could envision some of the local entertainers hiding away in the booths hoping not to be noticed. We had a wonderful dinner with some very fine red wines. Manuel said that he was glad that I was able to join them, he wanted to talk with me about an opportunity for advancement. He said that he had not been happy with the Manager of the Airport office. Manuel had recently been made aware of some inappropriate transactions that had been uncovered by the auditor from New York. The manager had been escorted out of the office on Friday by the auditor. The Auditor felt that the assistant manager that had worked with him would not be the appropriate choice to replace him. The auditor felt that someone fresh and not connected to any staff member there would be a good choice. I was suggested by Manuel to be the replacement and they decided to offer me the position as the Manager at the airport branch. It was so unexpected that I was clearly stunned and appreciative at the same time. I thanked him for the offer and I told him that I would accept and that I would do my best that I could for him and the company.

The very next day Manuel asked Kamuela from the Waikiki office and Margie the assistant manager from the airport to meet with him. The meeting became very intense as Margie was very confrontational with Manuel about inappropriately letting the manager go. She had worked by his side for years and he did not deserve to be released. She said that she was the assistant and she deserved to have the manager position. I could see Manuel's' cheeks quiver as he addressed Margie. He looked directly at her and told her that the decision has been made and he was happy to have her continue as the Assistant Manger with me being the Manager. The choice was hers and he expected her decision by the end of the day. With that he thanked her for coming and requested that she return to the Airport branch for the day.

Manuel though that it would be best that we continue our meeting at a nearby restaurant. Most of the breakfast crowd had moved on to work and the restaurant was very quiet. We ordered our coffee, pastries, and fruit. There was a sense in the air that we needed to chit chat a bit to let the tensions of the morning's interactions rise and be swept away with the trade winds.

I was informed that I would spend the next two weeks with Kamuela to observe and shadow her while learning the skills of running a small office. The Waikiki office was nothing like the airport office in appearance, but the business activities were very similar. Kamuela's assistant manager would be temporarily assigned to the airport branch as acting manager until I was ready to take over. I was thrilled with the decisions that Manuel had put into place. I enjoyed Kamuela and I could walk to work in about five minutes. Perfect time for all of this to happen I thought.

The training went very well, I learned a tremendous amount from Kamuela, and I was ready to head out to the airport. Kamuela, Patty, and myself were asked to meet with Manuel on Monday morning. We talked openly about how my training had progressed and Patty shared about the intense bitterness that Margie had towards the company. Margie who was Filipino, and the manager who was Filipino felt that it was the fault of the *haoles* (Manuel and myself) that things played out as they had. She felt they had been discriminated against. Patty was concerned as to how I was going to be accepted at the airport. She felt that Margie may have such deep feelings she may want to sabotage my position. Manuel was quiet for a short time and said that the plans that he had in mind would need to be altered a bit. He and Marcella were going to be leaving for Rome for three weeks. Marcella had been invited to have a private audience with the Pope and she was not going to turn that down. They would be leaving the week before Christmas and returning the week after New Year's Day. They would be staying at the Pension Di'Giglioni which is a small hotel that they had stayed at for years. He said that he did not want to have to worry about my transition at the airport and he was going to leave things as they were for now. We would begin the new year with a new vision. He said that may or not include Margie. He was going to call one of attorneys in the New York Office to discuss Margie's indirect allegations. Kamuela and I stood up to return to the Waikiki office,

Manuel said, "Oh and by the way Chet, I would like you to take the company car home with you? I would also like you to go the airport several times during the week to have your presence felt. I said that I will be certain do that."

Arrivederci.

My first visit to the airport office was the following Wednesday. When I arrived, Margie was the only one in the office. She was waiting on a customer and very much ignored my presence. The office had teller windows behind glass and a security entrance that had an electronic buzzer that needed to be pushed to allow entrance. After the customer left, I approached the window and greeted Margie.

"Hello Margie, it is good to see you. Would you please buzz me in."

She said, "I need to see your airport security ID to let you in."

"I do not have an airport identification. I will surely acquire that on before my next visit."

"That is fine," she said. "I will see you next time and buzz you in with adequate identification."

My initial thought was to challenge her self-inflicted authority. I thought better of that. I returned to the Waikiki office just in time for Patty to call me from the airport office. She said that Margie had told her about not letting me in and Patty had told her that she was being insubordinate to me as Manager.

Margie said to Patty, "I am going to lunch, you can address the issue of being insubordinate to the two *haoles*." Patty, Kamuela, and I agreed to let it blow over, and in my future trips to the Airport I would go when Patty was there. I said, "Patty, by the way do you have an airport ID?"

"No, but I do have a key and I will have one made for you."

❀ ❀ ❀ ❀ ❀

Christmas was right around the corner. I decided that I should host a cocktail party in my apartment for a few of the staff at Deak Perera. It would be complicated in deciding on who to invite. I decided to invite the staff members with whom I had formed a social as well as a work connection with. It would also be a going -away party for Christine. She was leaving Deak Perera and the Islands to follow her new boyfriend to the mainland. I would make a guest list and then pair it down to a reasonable amount of people to have in my small living space. I was going to have the party on a night when Jackie and Paul would be working and I would not invite Paul's sister Diane and Glen.

On Sunday December 22, 1974, I had a gathering of six staff members and their significant others. It was a beautiful evening with light trade winds blowing and Waikiki was lit up for the Christmas season. Many of the buildings were decked out with additional holiday lighting that glittered back at us on the *lanai*. I did not have to decorate my apartment for the holidays—the view took care of the need for that. We shared cocktails and stories of our lives before Deak Perera had brought us together. I was on cloud nine.

I wanted to allow the opportunity for Manuel to be a part of our celebration. He is the reason that we all have the opportunity to share our time together. He introduced me to this wonderful group of people. There is nothing like that warm and fuzzy feeling from an unexpected call from someone that you care about, and I cared very much about him. He gave me strength, and most of all a passion for life and for work, I wanted to give him a surprise.

I did some checking with a local telephone operator while I was at work about how to call Rome, Italy and how could I find the telephone number for the *Pension Di'Gigglioni*. She was extremely helpful, she called for overseas information and they gave her the telephone number, she gave me dialing instructions and said that if I called at 9 pm Hawaii time it would be 8 am in Rome the following morning. I wrote it all down and I thanked her for her time and I wished her a Merry Christmas.

I told my guests that I was going to call Rome in the hopes of us all being able to speak to Mr. VanGeldern in Rome. They were stunned that I knew the name of the hotel, more stunned that I had the telephone number and that I knew how to complete the call. It all went as planned. After dialing the number it took several minutes for a strange buzz buzz buzz that was calling Rome. I was lucky that the person answering at the *Pension Di'Gigglioni* spoke fluent English.

"May I please speak to Mr. Manuel VanGelderen."

He said, "Of course you can see him and Marcella is in the garden room having coffee, may I tell him who is calling?"

"No I would like it to be a surprise."

When Manuel answered, "*Ciao*," all of us in my small apartment loudly said, "Merry Christmas." Manuel was stunned, he said his favorite Croation swear words "*Yi Bemti Boga.*" It was truly what the Christmas spirit is all about.

After everyone left, I sat alone on the *lanai* and I gave thanks for all of the opportunities that I have had during my brief time in these beautiful islands. I decided that it was a perfect time to take a few puffs...

Chapter Eleven

"HAU'OLI MAKAHIKI HOU"
happy new year

I had called my mom and dad after Thanksgiving to check in and fill them in on a bit of what I was doing. I had previously mailed them a full coconut. In Hawaii, you can pick up a dried coconut from the ground, write on it with a magic marker, address it and take it to the post office and mail it home.

My dad said, "The mailman Mr. Tate was amazed to see the coconut and he if I would have you mail him one as well?"

"That would not be a problem," I said.

I was pleased to hear that they sounded well. My dad said that my mother's brother Emil had been out to visit them and he had wondered if I had visited with his step daughter who lived in Kaneohe. I told him that I had not and I thanked him for the reminder to do that. I told them that I would be calling after Christmas day, as I was certain it would be easier to get a telephone line out of the islands. I wished them a Merry Christmas and that I missed them very much. There was security on both ends that I finally had a telephone and we had a way to connect with each other.

I decided to call my cousin Rosemary and say hello. I had only met her a couple of times so it was like reintroducing myself to her. She lived in Kaneohe with her husband Mark, who was in the Navy, and their three children. She asked if I could join them at their home on Christmas eve for dinner. I was thrilled with the opportunity to be with some family, even though I didn't really know them. I asked Paul if I could borrow his car to drive to Kaneohe and he said yes, as both Jackie and him would be working long hours over the Christmas holiday and he would not be needing his car on that day.

I had only driven a couple of times on the island. I had no sense of direction and the names of the streets had no grid whatsoever to guide me. I had taken the bus with Al to Kaneohe and I decided that I would actually follow the bus from Waikiki. It would take a bit longer but at least I would be going the right direction. Rosemary had given me directions to their home and I was quite certain I could find my way once I was in Kaneohe. I was invited to arrive at 3 pm to join them for cocktails and early Christmas Eve dinner. The drive over was so beautiful, the lushness of the tropical jungle on both sides of the Pali Highway was raw and beautiful. The water department had planted hundreds of Poinsettias that were all in full bloom along the roadway. I had not expected to see them in Hawaii, I had not known them to be a tropical plant. The view from the top of the Pali looking down onto Kaneohe bay was something from a postcard. I had to pinch myself to confirm that me and the scenery were both real. I kind of had to pinch myself often, a lot of my dreams were coming true.

I was greeted with warmth from Rosemary and Mark, I instantly felt a wonderful familial connection. Their children were introduced to me in their family room for a brief time and they all went back to their individual rooms. We had beautiful hors d'oeuvres and cocktails, we shared many stories about our families that had not previously been shared. I was invited to the dining room with a table that was beautifully laid out with formal dinnerware and a large floral centerpiece. There were only three place settings. I asked where were the children were going to eat. Rosemary said that the children preferred to eat separately when they had a formal dinner, as they get bored quickly and ask to be dismissed immediately after the salad had been served. That made sense. Several hours had passed and I felt that I should be heading back to Waikiki. I was a bit worried to be driving in the night. Mark asked me if I would be interested in having him purchase any alcohol for me at the base since it was a fraction of the cost of what I would pay in the stores. I said that I would love a case of Heineken beer. I offered to give him some cash and he said not to worry and that we could settle that when we meet again. I thanked them both for a wonderful Christmas Eve and I told them that I would call soon to have them over to my humble apartment with a spectacular view.

Driving out of their subdivision, everything looked very different in the dark. I was unsure of directions during the day and that was amplified in the dark. I had been careful to make mental notes of where to turn when I had driven over in the day light. All seemed to go very well until I got to Kamehameha Highway. There was a large division between both sides of the highway. Two lanes were going in either direction. I was in the turn lane, but when I attempted to enter the lane going towards the Pali Highway, I somehow turned too sharply and I was actually going opposite traffic going the wrong way. I immediately figured this out as there were headlights coming my way. I had time to quickly turn around but quickly was not in my favor. I turned right around and I rolled into the back of a car that was parked at the light. He jumped out of his car and he waved me over to the side of the road.

"I am so sorry for my poor driving skills," I said.

He said, "No problem Bra' no harm done to my truck." His bumper had put a dent in the top of the hood of Paul's VW but his truck had no signs of an impact. He told me how best to get back on the right road and head home. I was so thankful to have met a kind local man. All the way home I was trying to think of what to tell Paul. I decided that I would inspect the car in the morning and perhaps ask Al for a referral to someone who may be able to fix it.

I did just that the first thing in the morning when Paul was still sleeping. Al came over and when he looked at the car he said, "I don't know what you are worrying about, there is a small dent without any paint damage whatsoever." I popped the hood, Al pushed his hand on the inside to the hood and out came the dent. Thank God for the somewhat flimsy hood on his car. Other than Al's hand prints on the dusty hood, there was no damage. Wow what a miracle! I invited Al to jump in and I offered to buy him breakfast at Zippys. I would go to the car wash to have Paul's car detailed while we ate. Al said that there was a full service wash that was only one block from Zippys, that would work out perfect. We dropped the car off and I went for the full detail. It was more than I had intended to pay, but it was cheap knowing what price I would have had to pay if there had been more damage. I thought I had better stop pushing my luck and not do crazy things while driving someone else's car.

✸ ✸ ✸ ✸ ✸

I was ready for 1975 to begin, I felt like I had assimilated myself very well into the rhythm of the islands. I received a call from my cousin Rosemary Goldy and she said that her husband Mark had picked up a case of Heineken from the military base for me. She asked if they could bring it over to me in Waikiki, and I welcomed the idea. I suggested that we meet at Hulas Bar and Lei stand because Jackie had some visitors coming to our apartment that night so I would not the able to host them. They said that would be fine, they had not been to Hulas and they said that they were always looking for a new place to have visit and have a cocktail. I went to the bar a bit early so that I could acquire a table. The bar was located completely out of doors under a very large banyan tree. The only roof covering was over the service bar and there were several large umbrellas covering most of the tables. We sat at one of the tables for four and sipped local drinks and talked about their lives and what they did and did not like living in the Islands. Rosemary was fearful of flying and it was bothersome for her to have to fly to visit her mother in Utah. Mark said that he had only a couple of year's left until retirement and that they would most likely be returning to Kanab, Utah. I thought that was very strange wanting to live in the southern desert of Utah. Mark explained that he was born and raised there and his mother lived there in the family home. Mark said that his family had property that they had hopes of building a home on. As the nightly crowd funneled in, it was apparent that there were more single men than women or couples.

Mark said, "Chet, is this a gay bar?"

The question took me by surprise.

"You know I have not really thought of it in terms of that. I can see that there are a lot of men here tonight, I have only been here a couple of times early in the evening on my way home from work, and the occupants have been mixed."

Rosemary said, "I like it, we have never been to a gay bar before, thank you for suggesting that we meet here. There are certainly many handsome men here to look at and the music is great!"

I said, "We will have to meet here again soon. I'm glad that we have had some time together, and thank you for the Heineken beer, I will put it to good use. I'll save a couple of bottles for when you come to visit."

New Year's Eve came quickly and I had no plans. I decided not to go to the beach with all of the tourists and I would just hang out at the pool at the Four Paddle and have a relaxing day. I had only been to the pool a couple of times and I kept to myself and read my book. There were only a few people at the pool, two couples and one single man that I had noticed there on many of the weekends. He was very handsome and was perhaps of Hawaiian descent. I thought for a second of introducing myself to him and decided not to do that. I went back out to the apartment, showered and contemplated what I should do for dinner. I decided to walk down the next block and get a Tonkatsu Plate and bring it home. I opened one of the ice-cold Heineken beers from the fridge and went out on to the lanai. The sun was about to set and I swallowed the beer in just a few big gulps. I must be thirsty. I grabbed another beer and went back out to the lanai. I noticed that the handsome man who was at the pool earlier was back at the pool with a tray of beautiful Shish kebobs and he was getting the grill ready to cook. I didn't even think before I called down to him at the poolside. "I will trade you a Heineken beer for a kebab." He didn't linger with his response. "Yes of course that sounds like a good trade." I hurriedly grabbed four additional beers and I went down to the pool to join him.

"Hi," I said, "I'm Chet and I have noticed you here at the pool on the weekends, usually reading a book."

"Hello, I am Brandon it is nice to meet you, I have noticed you here at the pool, you also usually reading a book. I live in unit 902 and I spend most of my weekends here where it is quiet and not on the beach that is flooded with tourists. Thank you for the beer. I decided that I would eat before heading over to Kaneohe to join my family later tonight for a New Year's celebration."

I said, "Thank you for the offer of a kabob, I have no plans and I have nothing to eat so this is great. I live right below you in 702."

Brandon said, "I have seen you at the pool a few times and I notice that you seem to enjoy spending time out on your lanai. I am always amazed how few people spend time outside of their condos, I guess they all inside enjoying their air-conditioning.

We sat at one of the poolside table's and I was amazed that Brandon had paid so much attention to the presentation of the food that we ate. I thanked him for including me in his feast and I told him that I looked forward to sharing another beer with him. I wished him a Happy New Year, and I was almost envious that he was going to be with his family for a New Year celebration.

My ohana was growing and I was certain that I too would be going to a family celebration when the next New Year's Eve came around.

I grabbed my hidden baggie and I went out to the lanai. I had a few puffs and I watched the skies flash with fireworks and saw their reflections like stars in the ocean.

I was once again amazed that the outside elevator at the Sheraton Waikiki just kept going up and up and never reached the top. I wondered to myself if that was the stairway to heaven?

Chapter Twelve
"KO'U 'OHANA HAWAI'I"
my Hawaiian family

I found the joys of having a variety of different types of *ohana*, I had my *haole* roommates and I am forever grateful to have had this opportunity to be in Hawaii with them. We had very little in common but we had respect for each other's privacy. Even though we lived in a very tight space, our work schedules allowed each of us time alone. I have thought that perhaps I had seen a bit of a romantic interest from Jackie toward Paul. I knew very little about either one of them. I was aware that they both went their separate ways to the beach. Paul would normally drive somewhere out of Waikiki, I did not ask him where he went and he did not offer where he was going. Jackie would head out to the beach in front of the Sheraton Waikiki and lather herself up with her baby oil. The both had tans that would make any of the suntan oil companies proud. I would head to the edges of Queen's beach on Saturdays and Sundays, always alone. I liked having the time to recharge from the work week and read. The beach had a large grassy area that provided comfort of not getting covered with sand while still lying by the ocean. I would normally lie there if I did not intend to swim. A few times I would notice Diane and Glen with other friends, I would not impinge on their group, and I wasn't worried about being recognized by them as I was always wearing my moustache.

I would look down at the pool from my *lanai* on weekends and if I saw Brandon at the pool, which was normally on a Sunday, I would grab my book and head down to join him. Brandon was an avid reader and we would discuss the books that we were presently read-ing. We would briefly take about our private lives, being careful not to feel forced to answer too many questions. Brandon would often bring a variety of snacks to share, his food always looked like he had taken a lot of time getting it ready to present it at the pool. I would always take liquid refreshments with plenty to share with Brandon.

Easter Sunday was coming up and Brandon asked, "Would you be interested in joining my family for an early dinner in Kaneohe?"

"Oh, I'd definitely like to meet your family. Is there something that I could bring?"

"That won't be necessary, but perhaps you could make some-thing that you would normally make for Easter at your home."

I initially thought of making *Pavitica* (rolled walnut roll) but de-cided that I definitely did not have the baking tools that would be required to make that, so I decided on bread. My mother was a great baker and often times I would tail along with her and watch her bake. I was successful in learning a few things that she made well. I decided to make a *focaccia*.

❀ ❀ ❀ ❀ ❀

Good Friday was a holiday that was observed at Deak Perera and the office was closed. I was surprised to see Brandon at the pool when I was heading out for the beach. I changed course and went down to the pool instead.

"Hello Brandon, I was surprised to see you at the pool today."

"I should say the same thing back to you, I am guessing that we both have Good Friday off? I work for the Schuman Carriage Motor company, the owner is very good at observing all holidays whether they are Federal holidays or not. The company has been in the same family for almost 100 years and my father and I both work there. I am in their sales department for Cadillac and Subaru cars. In fact, my father went to Japan and was responsible for importing the first Subaru automobiles from Japan to the Islands."

"Thats great, I can't wait to meet him on Sunday."

"Who do you work for, Chet?"

"I work for a Deak Perera, a foreign currency exchange company. It is a great job with wonderful people."

Brandon said, "I know that company, I see it when I walk through the Outrigger Hotel on the way to the beach."

"Yes that is the same company. I've been working in the main office downtown and I was recently promoted to be the manager at the Airport Branch."

Brandon said, "I guess I know where we need to go to exchange our money when we go to Japan."

I wondered if I was hearing things or dreaming of things that would yet come to pass. Did he just say WE? I decided not to question what I thought Brandon had just said, and I just let it pass.

We spent the day together at the pool getting to know each other a bit more, and he suggested that I join him at his condo for dinner that night.

Brandon said, "I would like to prepare and share some local delicacies with you."

"That would be great I will see you around 7 pm and I will bring a bottle of wine."

A few minutes after 7 pm, I walked up two floors to his apartment. I was so thankful that Jackie and Paul were at work and that I didn't have to share the destination of my outings with them.

Brandon answered his door in a brightly colored Hawaiian shirt and white shorts. His legs were tanned, he had a terrific thick moustache and he was barefoot. He invited me to leave my flip-flops at the door. He explained that in Hawaii most homes do not allow shoes to be worn inside, and it is customary to see lots of shoes on the doorsteps of the homes.

The table was set beautifully, there was an amazing amount of interesting food on the table. We opened the bottle of wine and sat on the *lanai*. I felt electric, I felt the *aloha* spirit; it truly is one of unconditional love with an outpouring and receiving spirit among others. Brandon was someone very special and his giving of his spirit and sharing his culinary talents with me was incredible. We enjoyed a feast of foods that Brandon had to describe in detail. We had a very large platter of Sashimi (raw red tuna), Korean Kalbi, soyu chicken, miso soup, pickled radish, and white rice. I was curious as to when he had the time to complete all of the dishes after he left the pool. We talked with each other like we had known each other for a long time. I asked about his skills in preparing the food. Brandon talked about his attendance at Kamehameha High School, an education which included manners of dining and setting of the table. We cleaned up the table and sat on the sofa looking out at Waikiki. There was something that was happening between the two of us. I felt his eyes piercing right though me and I had a comfort level that I could not explain. I was sitting next to someone that God intended me to be with. The laws of attraction seemed to be in place between two men. Brandon had talked about a double date that he had been on with his friend Chuck's wife, and Brandon's date Lynnette. He had talked about a woman name Janice that he had dated in high school whose family owned and ran a small golf course in Kaneohe. There was no mention of any men in his life. I hadn't had either a man or a woman to share my story with him because there simply wasn't one. I felt that I had walked into Brandons life like I had always lived there, like my heart was a home just built for him. We talked all through the night until the sun began its journey across the sea. As I got up to leave, Brandon asked if he could give me a hug. I held tight until he let go. Hugging is the most beautiful form of communication that allows the other person to know beyond a doubt that they matter. I knew that it was Brandon that mattered to me.

I did not go back to my apartment, I went straight to the beach. As I walked along the shore, I saw a group gathering on the beach in front of the St. Augustine by the Sea Catholic Church. I had been to services there several times and I recognized the priest Father

Akiona. I joined in realizing that they were just beginning a sunrise service. It was a celebration signifying the scenes of Christ's followers that were outside his tomb, waiting for his resurrection. As they ministry came out of the church singing in unison and walking toward the shore, I went to my knees and sobbed. I had been reborn. I wanted to beg for God's understanding and his support of my life as it would begin in Brandon's arms. I somehow felt he could understand what I myself was not able to understand.

❀ ❀ ❀ ❀ ❀

We drove out to Kaneohe on Easter Sunday in the early afternoon, I had baked two delicious looking loaves of bread to gift to Brandon's family. He was right, there were many pairs of flip flops on the front porch. We walked in and I could see many of his *ohana*, laughing, talking, eating, and having fun in each other's company. Brandon's mother, Dawn, was in the kitchen; she came forward and gave Brandon a hug and a kiss, she leaned into me giving me a kiss on the cheek.

"*Aloha*," she said. "Welcome to our home. I am so happy you could come, Brandon has spoken very highly of you." I am sure that my face was again the color of my first sunburn.

"Thank you for the invitation, I made some bread for you and your family this morning. I cannot hold a candle to Brandon's cooking but I can make a decent loaf of bread."

"Yes, Brandon is an excellent chef and his presentation is the best on the islands. I am certain he will be willing to teach you a few things."

"I am sure of that, I am thankful to have met him, we live only two floors apart at the Four Paddle."

We went out to the patio and we were greeted by his father, Earl. With his beer in one hand and a cigarette in the other, he gave me a hug and said I am pleased to meet you. His smile was intense and the slight gap between his two front teeth added to his handsome character. His laughter was infectious and welcoming. The introductions were plenty, his sisters, brother in laws, nieces, nephews, grand babies, any others in his extended family. I was overwhelmed with the love and sharing that I saw in this family. I soon had a cold Primo beer in my hand and the other hand was dipping into the poi. They laughed as I said that was interesting and that I liked it.

Dawn said, "My family likes it when I make the poi because it is a wee bit sour. Poi is mixed with water using your hands, the mixture takes on a flavor from the person that has mixed it. It is a staple of our culture, you should try it with some of the grilled *Aku* bone, it is delicious together."

The day, the food, the family, the joy, the culture, their acceptance of me, it was all delicious. Brandon suggested that we should leave a little earlier than the family was ready to accept. He explained that we needed to drive back to Waikiki and that we both needed to work in the morning.

We arrived back at the Four Paddle and I got in the elevator first. Brandon pushed number 9,

I said, "Oh you forgot that I am on number 7."

He said, "You were..."

My heart said with pride, "This is impossible."

"It is risky," said my inexperience.

"It is pointless to resist," said reason.

"Give it a try," whispered my heart.

It has been said, "Don't find love, Let love find you. That's why it's called falling in love because you don't force yourself to fall. You just fall."

What was I going to say to Jackie and Paul when I went back to the apartment to get ready for work? I was hoping not to disturb them and they would stay asleep. But when I ended up going back to the apartment, they were not sleeping, they were sitting at the counter having coffee.

Paul said, "What is up with you, we have been worried. It is not like you to not let us know where you are?"

"I'm sorry I should have let you know, but I came back late from Kaneohe and I stayed at Brandon's."

Paul's lips curled and his eyes bulged looking back at me.

"You stayed overnight with Brandon in his apartment? How in the hell did that happen?"

I said, "I actually thought it would give you and Jackie some alone time without me here."

Jackie said, "Alone to do what? Perhaps we all need to have a long talk on our day off this Wednesday."

"That's a great idea," I said. "I have to catch the bus in 10 minutes, I will see you Wednesday."

Paul reached out towards me almost as if he wanted to strike me. I felt so much heat coming from him that felt he could burn my skin. It was time to run out of the door. Martin Luther said, "For where God built a church, there the Devil would also build a chapel."

I was ruffled by the situation that I left behind as I boarded the bus. I felt like I should just jump back off and move out. I had to think. When I got to the airport office, I had a half an hour until the staff would arrive. I called the Schumann Carriage company and I asked for Brandon Fernandez. They said that they would see if he had arrived yet. In a few minutes I heard his voice. I almost could not hold it together. I apologized for calling and I told him that I was very upset with my roommates' interactions this morning and I asked if I could come by his apartment after work and have him help me figure out a few things.

He said, "Chet, I was there for you last night and I plan on being there for you from now on."

"Thank you, I will see you tonight."

What did he mean "from now on"? Was I making things up and hearing what I want to hear? I was not certain. I had a job to do, I needed focus for that today and I had the safety of Brandon's support to help me figure things out starting tonight.

It was easy to pretend that I was not a mess, my mind wandered, I paced to and from the employee lounge, I drank way too much coffee and I was exhausted when I boarded the bus for the ride home. The bus ride that was always very quick was all of a sudden long and nerve -racking. The bus driver's announcements were too loud, the crazy tourists and all of their excitement was overwhelming.

When I arrived at the Four Paddle, I went to the fourth floor of the parking terrace. Paul had started driving his car to work after they gave him a free parking pass, I wanted to see if his car was gone, it was. I went to the apartment and I quickly changed my clothes and walked up to Brandon's apartment. Brandon greeted me with a hug and led me to the sofa. I shared with him the interaction that I had with Paul and Jackie that morning.

He said, "Chet I barely know Paul, but I think I know what is going on. Paul asked me to go to a movie with him a few months ago. I went with him and we went for a cocktail after the movie. I immediately felt that Paul was paddling the wrong direction. I left the bar and I told him that I was having to leave and meet my girlfriend at her condo on the Ala Wai. Since that time Paul has written me letters, he has left me gifts at my door, he has called me more than once and I had to tell him I was busy and I would appreciate it if we didn't have any further interaction with each other."

I said, "What did you do with the cards and gifts that he gave you?"

"I have them all in a bag in the closet and I have wanted to write him a kind note and place the bag at his door. I figured that since I met you, he would have given up."

"Oh my god, I had no idea, I didn't even think that he knew that you and I knew each other."

Brandon said, "One night last week when we were at the pool I saw Paul staring down at us from the *lanai*. I wanted to say something to you but I thought that there would be a time for that to happen."

"I don't know what to do. I have never had an intention of hurting anyone's feelings. I have seen very little of Paul and Jackie since we have moved into the Four Paddle. I don't even know what they do on their days off. I guess Jackie has been barking up the wrong tree with Paul as well."

Brandon said, "You have been sleeping on the floor in the same room with Paul for months and you did not know that he was gay?"

"The truth is I have actually not thought in terms of gay for anyone including myself. Perhaps I am extremely naive or perhaps I'm just accepting of everyone as they are without a label. This is very all very complicated."

Brandon said, "It does not have to be complicated. I fell in love with you when I first met you. I have never had this connection with anyone in my life. I look forward to being with you everyday and I would like you to move in with me and share everyday and night with each other."

I said, "I am very touched with your caring for me. The most wonderful thing that I have decided to do was to share my heart with you. Yes, I am ready to share my life with you as well. I fell in love with you because of a million tiny things that you didn't know you were doing. Things have been happening so quickly in my life, and all of them seem right."

Brandon went into the bedroom and came out with a bag. He said, "I have all of Paul's things, now let's go get yours."

We went to my apartment to get my personal things. I had very little to move. I made sure to take my plants that were given to me by Al's grandmother. I kept my keys and I left a note asking Paul and Jackie if I could meet with them the next day after work. Brandon set the bag for Paul next to my letter. I said to myself that tonight I have chosen to close the door to a bit of my past, open the door to the future, take a deep breath, step on through and start a new chapter in my life. *Aloha*...

The following day after work I went directly to my recently vacated apartment to meet with Jackie and Paul. Out of some strange, need for respect I knocked on the door. With no expressed reason to enter, I opened the door with the keys that I had kept. I called out for Jackie and Paul and there was no response. The door to the *lanai* was open which gave me pause to think that perhaps one of them was in the bathroom. I walked toward the open door and I looked into the bedroom and I saw Paul on his bed. He was not moving. I saw several pill bottles on the makeshift box that was his bed stand. I ran in and realized that Paul was still breathing but not moving. I shook him and I begged Paul to wake up. He opened his eyes and they seemed to be rolling around in circles in his head. He said, "I have done something stupid." I ran upstairs praying that Brandon was at home. We returned and Paul was still lying motionless. We lifted Paul up and propped his arms around our necks and took him to Brandon's car. Fortunately Brandon's car was a larger Buick with a full back seat. We laid Paul down and we rushed to The Queen's Hospital emergency room. I ran in and told the attendant that we had a potential overdose victim and we needed a gurney and assistance to get him in. They jumped into action and transported him quickly into the emergency room. The assistant asked me to fill out paper work for Paul. I didn't have much to put down other than his address, telephone number and contact information for Paul's sister, Diane. She reviewed the form and asked for his insurance information. I told her that I did not think that he had insurance, but I was not certain. She asked what my relationship to Paul was and I said there was none.

The assistant was able to get in touch with Diane, and shared with me that she would be here shortly. The doctor came out to the waiting area and took me into a small conference room. He said, "I pumped Paul's stomach, if you had not found him and brought him here his life would have ended, we will be keeping him overnight for observation. Do you know why he had taken all of the pills."

I said, "I have some ideas but that would be best left for Paul to share. I hope that you will give him some mental health observation as well as physical observation."

At that moment Diane walked in. She looked at me in the eye and she said, "You did this to him."

I felt the pain that she intended to inflict on me and I stood up and I said, "I will leave you with the doctor."

Unfortunately, for me the friendships that I made at the bank in Utah were taken away from me as quickly as they were made. There was no apology that I needed to make.

Brandon and I got in his car to go home and I cried the whole way home. I was thankful that my home was now with him.

❋ ❋ ❋ ❋

I thought that my short story with Paul had ended, but it had not. I had been introduced to a friend of Pauls who was taking a semester at the University of Hawaii. Shawna had been in Hawaii for about a month when I first met her. Shawna called me after she had heard about the incident with Paul, she was sorry to hear about the situation. She said, "I hope you remember about our trip to Kauai over the 4th of July." I didn't have the honesty in me to say no, but I had completely forgot about that. We had made plans to go to Kauai together. I had not been there and she wanted to go there, so we decided to join forces and go together. We agreed to meet the next day for coffee to discuss our plans.

I sat down with Brandon and explained the situation. He was very understanding and suggested that I follow through with my commitment to Shawna. He said that I would give her a sense of safety to travel along her side. Shawna was recently divorced from her husband and the islands were providing her with a movement forward after leaving a severely abusive marriage.

So off we went. We had already booked a room near the Nawiliwili harbor that was very close to the airport. We had a small rental car, a map, and a joyful sense of adventure in both of us. We immediately went to the hotel and decided that on our first day we would explore what was close to our hotel room. When we entered the room to drop off our bags neither one of us said a thing about the ONE double bed that was in front of us. We headed out for a short drive to *Wailua* Falls. The doubled-tiered waterfall clearly gave us a glimpse of this small fantasy island. Next, we drove to the Menehune Fish ponds. Legends say that a small race of people known as Menehune built the ponds 1,000 years ago. The ponds are the most significant fishponds on Kauai. We looked down at the ponds and the wide variety of birds that were enjoying their lush Hawaiian home. The light of day was beginning to dim and we decided to return to the hotel for our evening out.

I had read about the infamous Club Jetty that had opened in 1946. Club Jetty had become a leading night spot. Entertainers came from Las Vegas, local entertainers such as the famous Kui Lee and the Kingston Trio had performed there as well. Celebrities were known to have frequented the club while they were anchored on their yachts in the *Nawiliwili* harbor. We walked past the club and went on to our dinner at a small restaurant on the shore.

Nighttime comes quickly in the islands, with the sun setting just after 5:30 pm, the clubs are raring to go early in the evening. We walked into an empty Club Jetty. The sign on the front door said "Club Jetty, No Tank Tops, No Shorts, No bare feet." The inside looked like an old Bogie movie, fans were spinning overhead, and the tables were formica-topped. We were welcomed with an *Aloha* and handed the Happy Hour Menu.

We quickly decided on the 1/2 price drink of the day, the Mai Tai. The server told us that the entertainers would begin in another hour. They had a female group from Korea that was performing that evening. The Mai Tai's went down a bit too fast. I felt like if you could drink a sunset, this is what it would taste like.

When the trio came onto the stage wearing bits of glitz barely covering their bodies, Shawna and I were cheering like we were at a Rolling Stones Concert. We laughed, danced, and we were crazy enough not to worry about our behavior because no one knew our names. The Mai Tais didn't show us the way home, but they provided for a walk to the hotel that we would not remember in the morning.

The remainder the visit to Kauai was filled with additional fun and adventure. We tried to visit all of the places on the island that any tourist would do. We left out all of the worries of what we would be returning to in Honolulu. Brandon picked us up at the airport and we took Shawna to the University of Hawaii student housing. We hugged and we both silently knew that we would never see each other again. "*Aloha* my dear friend Shawna," I said as I saw her walk away pulling her suitcase behind her.

I was only home from Kaui for only two weeks when I received a call from Dorothy, a girl that I had lived next to at the University of Utah. She said that she was coming to Hawaii in two weeks and she asked if she could stay with me. I told her that I was staying in Brandon's apartment and that there would not be any room for her to stay. Dorothy showed up in Hawaii not just for the trade winds, she came for me. Brandon and I picked her up at the airport and we told her that her hotel was only two blocks away. We took her to the hotel that she had booked and said that we would like to visit with her over the weekend.

I was shocked to look down at the pool area from our apartment two days later and there was Dorothy with Paul and Jackie down by the pool. What the Hell, how in Hell, what was all of this about. I choose not to go to the pool. The sun had just set and there was a knock at our door. It was Dorothy and she was severely drunk. I stepped out into the hallway with her and she said that she had come over to the Four Paddle to surprise me and she was at the front door trying to figure out how to get in when Jackie and Paul came home from the beach. She told them she was her to see me. They said you need to come to the pool with us so that we can tell you the rest of the story. Dorothy insisted that she come in and meet Brandon and stay the night with us. I said to her that will would not be happening. "You can go down two floors and stay with your newly made friends Jackie and Paul." I walked backwards through the door and shut it leaving Dorothy in the hallway. An hour or so had passed and we were out on the *lanai*, I looked down and Dorothy was in one of the pool lounges sleeping. I figured Jackie and Paul had gone to work when she went back to their apartment so she just decided to return to the pool. Brandon and I decided that we could not leave her there alone, so we went to the pool and we woke her up and told her that we were going to walk her back to her hotel. She initially was a bit resistant but we insisted that we needed her to leave. We stopped at a small local diner that was on the way to her hotel, thinking that perhaps some hot coffee and a bit of food would help her. When her bowl of soup was put in front of her, she dropped her head directly into the soup. I grabbed her head and pulled it back upright, fortunately the soup was only warm. I wiped her face just in time for and eruption of vomit to come flowing out of her mouth. I was so disgusted, embarrassed, angry, humiliated, and most of all so unhappy that Brandon had to witness this from a person that presented herself as my good friend. We walked her to her hotel, we turned and walked away, I whispered to myself, "*Aloha* my former friend Dorothy. We shall not meet again."

The bad luck of three strikes came soon. Another girl that I knew from high school was on her way to visit me! The superstition goes "If three soldiers lit their cigarette from the same match, one of the three would be killed." This third visitor could very well take me to end of my wits. I decided to be kind and understanding and not take it all too seriously. That all worked until I went to Maui with Debbie, similarly as when I had gone to Kauai with Shawna. Shawna and I had slept in the same bed and we didn't even notice each other. Debbie on the other hand was convinced that once I was in bed with her, I would be hers. The first overt touch from her, I pulled away and said we need to talk. I told her that I was in love with Brandon and this simply cannot be. I grabbed my suitcase, I told her that I would be leaving on the last flight back to Honolulu. I told her to check with the front desk to help her book an island tour of Maui. I whispered to myself, "*Aloha* my former friend Debbie. We shall not meet again." Debbie called two days later asking if I could take her to the airport. It was easy to say no in an honest way, I did not have a car. I gave her directions for catching the bus and I wished her well. She said, "I am sorry Chet..."

Chapter Thirteen

"ALOHA KE KAHI KA KAHI"
love one another

The music of Hawaii is enchanting, there is a transcendent quality and something very grounded in it. It is very roots-oriented and it grabbed a hold of me so much that it changed the way that I listened to music. I not only heard it, I felt it in my soul.

Brandon and I went back to Kaneohe to visit with Dawn and Earl on a Saturday afternoon. I asked Brandon if I could take his car to run down to the Kaneohe Foodland, I wanted to buy some items to add to the Pu Pu's that we were going to be having. He said, "Of course, don't get lost."

The Foodland market was located in a small shopping center on the outskirts of town. I parked around back and noticed a group that was gathered in the small courtyard that was adjacent to the front of the stores. I could hear melodic Hawaiian Music coming out from the center of the courtyard. I went to see the group that was playing this melodic music with perfect harmonic voices. I was amazed that all of the guys playing were large-bodied. There was a small poster that said, *"The Makaha Sons of Ni'ihau."* Wow! Their voices and their music was a large as their bodies. I was completely awestruck at the whole event that I was watching. I returned to Dawn and Earl's place and described the band that I had just seen. They said almost in unison, "Welcome to Hawaii you have just experienced music Hawaiian style."

We were invited by Brandon's sister Bonnie and her husband Tommy for a birthday celebration of their aunt *"Tutu* Hanna" later that afternoon. I had an excitement and a nervousness at the same time. There were so many family members and I had to try and remember their names and not come across as the dumb *haole*.

We drove a short distance to Kahaluu, down a small narrow path to the edge of the shore like we were heading back to the old Hawaii. We walked down a steep incline to a small shack that was right on the shore of the ocean. This was the little grass shack scenario that I had in my head when I first came to Hawaii. No matter how many beautiful pictures you see, it doesn't come close to being here in person. You don't see Hawaii, you experience it.

The home was very weathered and a bit tired. The view and location of their home far overshadowed the tethered look of the shack. We entered the home from a small door that was under the main part of the home. Bonnie and Tommy greeted me with a warmth that cannot be communicated, only felt. There were no differences in our souls, the Hawaiian spirit of *Aloha* brought us together as one family. The children all came to greet Brandon as Uncle, and they gave me the same respect. We sat on the sofa and shared bits of information about each other. I noticed as I looked around that the floor was actually dirt. Tommy and Bonnie explained that they could not live upstairs as it was not safe. They had intentions of repairing the structure and moving back upstairs in the future. We were invited to a side patio area that was just feet from the ocean. There were a couple of wooden tables and benches, the tables were laden with a wide variety of food. I was introduced to many family members. The party was in honor of *Tutu* Hana who had turned 90 years old that day. She was a very small Hawaiian woman with a large smile. She was happily drinking her baby Miller beer in a bottle. She had a beanie on her head that was made of brightly colored yarn. I smiled at her and I assumed her beanie had a significance that perhaps I would not learn. Everyone was having a great time drinking beer, occasionally singing along with the music being played. Brandon's sister Aunty Erleen arrived and she was vibrant. She leaned over to show me an embroidered emblem that was on the jeans. She said, "How does my *Okole* look." I assumed based on her position that *Okole* was the Hawaiian word for buttocks. I said you look very nice. If I had been pinched by a needle, I would have burst with joy. My love for this moment and for Brandon was like a balloon, it was taking me as high as it could go, I was floating.

A few weeks went by and we were invited to a birthday celebration at a bar located at the Kaneohe Bayview golf course. The eighteen hole public course was designed by a family friend of Brandon's, Mr. Jimmy Ukauka and it was truly an Island Gem with beautiful views of Kaneohe bay.

All of Brandon's family were there minus the *keiki's* (children). I had only briefly met Brandon's sister Moana and it was fun to spend time with all three of his sisters. At the piano, a local entertainer, Mahi Beamer was singing. He seemed to know everyone in the crowd. Bonnie was a great dancer and she graced us with a couple of hulas, a few of them were a bit naughty, and we all had a joyous spirit amongst us. I made a mental note to talk to Brandon's family about securing an evening there for Brandon's birthday as a surprise.

The music of the islands was already in my blood, I sought after it in abundance. I took Brandon to see my favorite local entertainer *"Loyal Garner"* at the Ilikai Hotel. I did not think it could be any better than my first time there, it was now of a different color, I was in love with Loyal and her music, I was in love with Brandon, it was the best. That magic of *Aloha* was never to leave me. We attended the first of two shows that Loyal performed that evening, we left the hotel when the night was young. I suggested that since it was early and we had driven there, we continue the evening with a visit to a performance by *Jay Larrin*. I had met Jay when I had lived in the second of our transitional hotels. I would walk to the Ala Wai canal, I would have a dish of *saimin* under the bridge, and then I would walk to a hotel that was on the other side of the canal where Jay was performing. He was a transplant from Tennessee, his piano playing and music had a way of communicating with the tourists. He became one of the local celebrities that I followed and admired.

I invited Brandon's family to go to the Outrigger Hotel with us to see *Jay Larrin* perform at the lounge. Brandon had a great voice and he had written a song entitled "My Honolulu." I approached Jay on his break and asked him to invite Brandon to sing it to the audience. Jay called out to Brandon and he invited him to sing his song. Brandon looked me and told me I was crazy. He sang his song, it was great, the audience gave him a rousing applause. We gazed into each other's eyes and we knew that the bonding of our souls was priceless.

❋ ❋ ❋ ❋ ❋

I decided that I would love the opportunity to learn to play the Ukulele. Brandon said that his mother Dawn had gone to school with Sam Kamaka of the Kamaka Ukulele company. He would ask her if she could facilitate getting us Ukuleles. A few weeks later we had two beautiful Koa Soprano Ukuleles. Brandon already had a few basics down, but I was completely green. We enrolled in a class at the University of Hawaii for beginner Ukulele that was being taught by the locally recognized premier player, *"Ohto San." Ohto San* had played in many Hawaiian venues, he recorded solo and group records on the A & M record label. It became very clear during the first class that I was clearly way over my head. Most of the students were local residents that seemed to be already familiar with some of the playing techniques of the Ukulele. I knew that I would need a tutor in addition to attending the lessons. I was successful in playing a few chords by the end of the class.

Brandon wanted me to meet his Grandmother Hazel. She had come to Hawaii from the mainland as an actress during the era of Silent Films. She met and married Hyrum Anahu who was one of the local BeachBoys, he was part of the group of beach boys that included the famous *Duke Kahanamoku*. Brandon's mother was her first child. Hazel went on to marry several times and gave birth to four girls and one boy. I loved the color of her history. Hazel's daughter Sonny Jean was married to a local restauranteur, Randy Lee. He owned the Willows restaurant in *Moiliili* that was a favorite spot for locals celebrating birthdays, weddings, and other events. It was known for its Hawaiian buffet, entertainment and open air dining. We were going to meet Hazel there for Sunday Brunch. Several family members joined us that day, and all the women were dressed in their beautiful flowing Muumuu's and they had flowers in their hair. I greeted Hazel with a kiss on the cheek and I saw a sparkle in her eyes when she saw Brandon. The event was magical, delicious local food, champagne, and of course a terrific Hawaiian group of performers and one vocalist. I felt like they were singing only for our table to enjoy. They radiated love and *Aloha* to the highest degree. It was a beautiful way to spend an afternoon with my new forever *ohana*.

So many things were happening so quickly, so many changes, good changes, so many new introductions, and in some ways a few new anxieties. Brandon was very comfortable to be himself with his family and with others that we would be around. I was also very comfortable and felt free to be myself and there were never any questions concerning our relationship. It was simple—they loved Brandon and they loved me. I had not introduced Brandon to any of my work family. I had not even spoken of him. I decided that I wanted Brandon to meet some of the most important people in my life. I asked Manuel and his wife Marcella along with our secretary Rosemary and her husband Al to join us for dinner. We juggled times and decided on a Saturday evening in two weeks' time. I started having tremendous anxieties. I wasn't even sure what the basis of the anxieties were. They anxieties seemed to double every day. The following week I could hardly even focus. On Wednesday, I was sitting at my desk and I called Rosemary who was only feet away from me at her desk. I said, "Rosemary I am dying, I don't know what to do." After a very brief conversation she said, "Let me give my Dr. a call for you." She arranged for an Appointment with Dr. Styonovich at the Staub Clinic. He was a Psychiatrist and he was willing to see me on Friday. Rosemary said that would be a good day because Mr. VanGelderen was in another island that day and I could take the company car.

"Hello I am Dr. Styonovich nice to meet you. Rosemary gave you the highest recommendation as a new client."

"Thank you for seeing me on such short notice."

He said, "That is no problem, I had a cancellation so your timing is perfect. And you are here because you are gay?"

I said, "Ah, oh, a, I don't know. I know that I am having severe anxieties and it is beginning to affect my work."

"That is okay Chet, there is most likely nothing wrong with you, your anxieties are common for a young person who has just found out who he truly is. Let's begin working on this today and I have no concerns all will end well."

I returned after a 90-minute session with Dr. Styonovich, I called Rosemary to thank her for saving my life. I came home with little yellow magical pills in my pocket. I was to take one of them when the anxieties became overwhelming. I took half a pill at the clinic and I felt very calm. I decided not to share my experience with Brandon, I was feeling very weak of spirit and I wasn't ready to share any of my many flaws with him. I read the pamphlet that came with the medication and I read of the dangers of the possibilities of addiction to the medication. I decided there and then that I would have them in my pocket and I would not take them unless it was completely necessary. That was the beginning of my addiction to having Valium in my pocket at all times. I was determined that I was not going to take a medication to cure what I knew was an illness in my mind and not in my bloodstream.

Manuel and Marcella were the first to arrive to our apartment. I took them on a tour of all 480 square feet of our apartment. When they looked into our bedroom Manuel said, "OH MY GOD MARCELLA THIS IS THE SAME BED!" I died inside, wondering what Manuel had meant. After pouring a large glass of wine for everyone, Brandon said that unbeknownst to him the bed was in the apartment that his grandmother Hazel had owned at 250 Ohua. Manuel and Marcella had looked at the apartment when they were looking to buy. They did buy Brandon's grandmother's apartment but they did not want the bed. Oh my hell, here was this great big eight foot wide round bed with a tufted giant head board. I could just hear their minds going. I foolishly began to show them that our two lounge chairs pulled out to single beds, suggesting that I slept on one of them. I would learn at a later visit to their home for dinner that nothing was going on in their minds about us and the bed. They had met my wonderful partner Brandon and there were no judgements, no ill thoughts, no questions, only cheerful thoughts that they were appreciative of a great meal with us.

I told Dr. Styonovich the story of our dinner guests and he said, "So can I have the valium back?"

"Not yet," I said. "Lets' chat about that next time."

We continued on with our regular sessions to include addressing my severe fear of elevators. We did several exercises, none of which were productive. I continued to keep my valium in my pocket. The anxieties had changed into a different animal. I started having very severe panic attacks. Dr. Styonovich referred me to a physician to have a full workup to ensure that I did not have anything medically wrong going on. I did not have any medical issues. I told him that it must be because of the spirit gum that I used to glue on my moustache. We both laughed, I was on my way to healing, but the healing still entailed having valium in my pocket....

Brandon decided that I needed to have a short vacation away. We went to the big Island of Hawaii. We were staying in Hilo and we would continue on around the island. We would to go the Volcano National Park and we would stay at the Volcano House. We stayed at a beautiful hotel on Hilo bay. We had taken the elevator to the top floor to have dinner in the restaurant that circled the whole top floor. There was floor-to- ceiling glass with a different vista from every angle. The Mauna Kea Volcano was encircled in snow and I had a hard time envisioning that it would ever get cold enough to snow. Our main entree was just delivered to our table when I started to have a severe panic attack. I told Brandon that I had to leave right away. How embarrassing for me, sad for Brandon to have to endure and no clear explanation as to why the present situation had caused the event. Sad to say the pill in my pocket now became the pill under my tongue. The events would happen sporadically and Dr. Styonovich was convinced that as my life matured and went forward the frequency of the events would slip away over time. I often wondered how could these anxieties exist within me in such a peaceful, beautiful environment. I was dying inside and no one knew it but me. I could best describe my feelings like it is halfway between feeling like I would faint, and feeling like I would die. The most frustrating thing about having a panic attack is knowing as you are freaking out that there's no reason to be freaked out, but lacking the ability to shut the emotion down. The best way I found to deal with the situation was to stay far away from discussing my affliction with anyone other than Dr. Styonovich and to begin visualizations of letting the anxieties melt away from my brain to my toes.

❀ ❀ ❀ ❀ ❀

I began to ride my bicycle more often by myself and also along with Brandon when he had time. I would walk the beach early in the mornings and late at night from Queen's beach to Ft. Derussey. Brandon had a dinner meeting with his colleagues on a Saturday night, so I decided that I would walk down Kuhio Avenue thorough the Waikiki Jungle and circle back to Kapahulu Avenue. I liked walking through the Jungle as it always gave me a sense of the old Hawaii. The jungle was a small bohemian enclave that was at the Diamond Head end of Waikiki. It was in stark contrast with the manicured shops and hotels closer to the sea. It was a low-rent area of one and two story cottages, small homes and apartments. Its denizens were a constantly shifting group of young people who were here temporarily from the mainland. They were there as if on a hiatus from their life, and were adopting a carefree lifestyle. Al had told me to stay away from the jungle at night. He said that some of the local hooligans liked to harass young *haoles* at night. I had just passed the last hotel on Kuhio Avenue and I was nearing Ohua street when I spotted three large local boys sitting on the bench at the bus stop. As I started to walk by them they jumped up,

"What are you doing here *haole* boy?" one of them said as he grabbed me by the arm.

I replied, "I am just walking through to Kapahulu Street to meet a friend."

He said, "If you want to make it there you had better give us your wallet, everything in your pocket and your watch."

Fortunately, I had left my wallet behind and I had only grabbed a few dollars to buy myself a plate of lunch on my way home. I gave them all that I had and just when I was starting to take off my watch, the bus appeared and stopped. The boys pushed me down to the ground and said you had better watch your back. The bus stopped and the driver came out and asked, "Are you okay?"

I said, "I am fine I am just a bit shaken up."

He suggested that I get on his bus and that he would drop me off outside of the jungle. I was sad for that event to have happened and realized it was good to take the advice of one of the locals and stay out of the jungle at night.

Sunday morning brought a new day and a new type of excitement. Rosemary and Mark had invited Brandon and I to go to the Polo games at *Mokuleia*. The Hawaii Polo Club was located on the pristine North Shore between the majestic *Waianae* mountain range and the clear waters of the Pacific Ocean. It provided a unique and exceptional venue for the game of kings to share the passion and lifestyle of the sport of Polo. The club attracted national and international spectators, including royalty such as Prince Charles. Rosemary asked us to join them at their house and we would ride together to the Polo field.

The minute I saw Mark and Rosemary come out of their house, I knew that Brandon and I clearly had not gotten the memo about the expected attire. Rosemary was dressed in a beautiful bright yellow sun dress with bright patterns of hibiscus. Her hat was equally as elegant but not as brightly adorned with patterns as her dress. Her stylish sunglasses and tasteful shoes finished off her ensemble. Mark had on white pants, white slip-on leather shoes without socks, and a bright tastefully patterned *Aloha* shirt. His hat and sun glasses finished out his outfit almost in unison with Rosemary's dress. Brandon and I had on *Aloha* shirts and shorts. We were obviously way underdressed. We got in the Mercedes Benz and we were handed a glass of champagne to have along the way. We pulled into a space along the fence surrounding the Polo field. Rosemary set out a beautiful blanket, Mark put chairs out, and out came baskets of food and drink fit for a Polo match. I definitely would not have expected this typically English event on the Islands of Hawaii. I was blown away when the announcer presented a welcome to the Royal Prince Charles. Rosemary and Mark had left that detail out. It was a wonderful surprise and it made this afternoon such a thrill. Attending the polo game was like wearing a fine old mink coat, opulent, dignified and warm, and yet we were in the islands where a mink coat would surely not appear on any of the attendees.

The following week we were invited to go the island of Maui and visit with Brandon's sister Erleen and her family. We chose to fly directly into Hana to save the five-hour drive from Kahului Airport to Hana. We booked seats on a small commuter airline, *Aloha Island Airlines*. I was a bit anxious when I saw that the airplane was a six-seater airplane. The Pilot invited one of us to sit in the co-pilot's seat. Brandon suggested that I should do that. The pilot handed me a headset so that I could hear the communication that he was having with the Honolulu airport. The view from the small aircraft as we flew over Diamond Head and along Waikiki was incredible. I felt very safe until we encountered a bank of clouds, I became very concerned because I wasn't able to see the islands. The pilot noticed my sense of concern and he explained that he could fly us safely into Hana without being able to see the islands. We broke out of the clouds as we headed down the coast of Maui towards Hana. Hana is one of the most isolated communities in the state with a population of less than 1,000. There is a picturesque road that winds along Maui's northern coast for 64 miles of lush coastline, waterfalls and a vast rainforest. The narrow road with 59 tight bridges and 620 curves is not for the faint of heart. I was happy to be on the small plane and not on the highway. The dramatic views of the bay and pier leading to the housing of the small town was like a postcard coming to life.

Erleen was waiting at the airport with her van filled with her children. They were so excited to see their Uncle Bran and they were quick to give their *Aloha* to their new Uncle Chet. We had been welcomed to stay with Erleen and her family, I asked Brandon if we could please stay somewhere with our own sleeping room. One of Erleen's friends offered us a small private room with a bath that she rented out to tourists who arrived in Hana only to realize that they did not want to drive back to Kahului the same day. We dropped off our small bags and we drove to Erleen's home. Their home was located on the large 4500 acre Hana Ranch. The ranch houses were small with single walls of wood and metal roofs. Each of the homes had an outdoor covered parking that was used as an outdoor living space. Erleen's husband Dado greeted us with smiles and hugs. Dado was Filipino, he worked as a butcher at the Hana Ranch Store that was next to the Hasegawa General Store. Dado told us in a very severe pidgin English that we were going to have steaks for dinner that he had just butchered that day. I was at a loss to most of what he was saying, but I could tell that he was saying it with love. The children were a joy to be with, they were polite, inquisitive about who I was, and so wonderfully naive about the mainland. After several mini Miller beers I started to relax, and the magical little pills didn't have to come out of hiding in my pocket. Dado started the barbecue and he put something on top of the grill that I could not even begin to guess what it was. He took some of it off the grill and I could see a white liquid oozing out of the long tuberous meat. He said,

"Chet come try, Ono you know."

"Can I ask what it is?"

"You can after you have a taste."

I took a piece and put it on my plate. As I cut into it a cottage cheese type of substance came out. Erleen explained that I was eating the udder of the cow. The substance that was coming out was milk. She said the Hawaiian name that was something like "Now I You." That was the first of the Hawaiian delicacies. Next came the *Opihi*. They are limpets that lives on the seaside rocks and they are notoriously hard to pry off. You remove the shell eating them either raw or cooked. In Hawaiian culture, it is a prized delicacy. It is eaten to celebrate a special occasion or birthday. I put one in my mouth and I tasted the ocean, briny and sweet with a distinct snap, crunch, and bounce. There is a Hawaiian saying: "*He ia make ka opihi*" (*Opihi* is the fish of death). It is because people risk their lives for the taste of *Opihi*, being swept out to seat while attempting to pick them off the rocks. It is easy to see why the Hawaiians refer them as "*Onolicious.*"

The steaks were grilled to perfection and the meat seemed to melt in our mouths. This Hawaiian Paradise was so simple yet so refined, so honest, so real, and foremost it was most loving.

We joined the *keiki's* to go swimming at the Hana bay pier. The pier was used in the past for freighters to be loaded with sugar to carry Hana's sugar crop to the rest of the island. The water around the pier was deep and the pier seemed to tower above the water. The *keiki's* had no fear as they jumped from the pier into the waves that were crashing into the pier. It had to grab all my strength to let go of my fear as I jumped in. I felt an amazing rush of fear, excitement, and ultimately a sense of peace from the warm Hawaiian waters enveloping my body. One of the young boys Keoni asked me, "Uncle do you know everybody in the mainland?"

I said, "No the mainland is very large, it would be impossible to know everyone there. I bet that you are lucky to probably know everyone in Hana."

I was told by Erleen that the night before Keoni wanted to know more about my relationship with Brandon. She told Keoni to think of Brandon and I as he would think of a couple like boyfriend and girlfriend. She said that he seemed to understand our love for one another and said, "Oh okay."

We showered and changed for lunch and I put on a shirt that I had purchased from a thrift store in Honolulu that was made from an old Hawaiian flour sack. Dado had on a very similar shirt, I told him that I liked his shirt and he said back to me, "but free dough." I thought perhaps that he was commenting to me about the flour sack shirt being dough, Brandon said, Chet he is saying that his shirt was free though! Out of the blue one of Erleen's daughters Tammi asked me if I wanted to have my feet massaged. I said of course, and she proceeded to give me a painful yet delightful Shiazu massage. I was so amazed at the strength in the hands of a little girl.

Erleen suggested that we drive out to the Seven Sacred Pools to go swimming. The pools were formed millions of years ago by a streamflow that flowed to the sea. The pools are surrounded by rainforests and waterfalls and they are perfect for swimming. The freshwater pools are definitely the best in all of Maui. Although the pools are called sacred, they are not actually sacred in any way. The actual name is the *Ohe'o Gulch*, and it is part of the Haleakala National Park. The name *"Ohe'o"* translates into "something special." That day will always remain in my heart as Sacred. We said our *Alohas* to our Hana family and boarded the small plane the next morning to fly back to Honolulu. As we flew up the coast of Oahu passing by Koko Head, Diamond head, and Waikiki—it was an image that can never be duplicated. Each time I saw the shoreline, it captured my heart and soul in a different glorious way. *Pomaika'i au*, blessed am I...

Chapter Fourteen

"E KOMO MAI NOU KA HALE"
come in make yourself at home

Brandon's mother and father were going to be going on an extended vacation to Mexico City and they asked if we would want to house sit while they were out of town. We jumped at the opportunity for the change of scenery. We had just recently adopted a beautiful cocker spaniel puppy that we called *"Elua,"* translated to mean the number two. We knew that *Elua* would love the opportunity to put her paws on the soil on the Windward side and run amongst the banana and papaya trees.

The windward side of Oahu is the East shore. It is about 30 minutes from Waikiki and it has a stark contrast to Waikiki and its high-rise hotels and apartments. The region is made up of quiet, coastal neighborhoods that are nestled between a stunning 3000-foot mountain range, the Ko'olau's and the sea. The quiet nature and lush beauty of the foliage was a dream come true for me. We settled into staying there and I felt completely at home. *Elua* too was ready to give up her hostage life of living in a condominium on the 9th floor and planting her feet firmly on the ground. I too felt the desire for that.

The first Saturday morning while staying at the home on Kahiko Street, Brandon had to go to work. I was sitting having coffee at the kitchen table and Brandon's uncle Jake walked past the windows of the patio. He looked in and he said to me, "Whose little girl are you?" I could not think of an immediate response, so I walked outside and shook his hand and I said I was a friend of Brandon's. He said nice to meet you, and he continued on to the back yard to gather a wheel barrow that he was there to borrow as if he was unaware of calling me a girl. I was at home in the islands and that was okay with me.

I had the opportunity to meet the next-door neighbors, Gladys and Charlie Azevido. They were a Portuguese couple that had lived next door to the Fernandez family since they moved in. They both had their own distinct accent and manner of speaking that actually complimented one another. I told them that I was amazed at the amount of avocados that were growing on their tree in their back yard. I told them of my lusting over the fruit, and Gladys said that she would be right back and she came out of the house with a bag full of beautiful ripe avocados. They welcomed me to ask for more at any time. I asked them about the papaya trees that seemed to be growing out of the asphalt on a vacant lot across the street. Gladys said that one of the Japanese neighbors would throw out his wet garbage onto the asphalt for the wildlife and the papaya seeds would sprout directly on the asphalt. I thought to myself about how magical all this raw beauty was. I noticed a vine that was growing on the fence in the front yard of Gladys and Charlies house. The psychedelic flowers looked like a beautiful specimen that seemed to be from another planet. The flowers were almost beyond description, resembling something one might see during a dream. The fragrant flowers had white petals that formed the base and on top of that, a vivid purple center streaked outwards from the center like fine whitish hairs. Gladys said that it was a *Lilikoi* vine and that I might know as passion fruit. She said that they would use the fruit that was produced from the vine for making jams, syrups, and juice.

We wanted to take the opportunity of living in the house to invite Grandma Hazel over for dinner. We could make use of the fruits that Gladys and Charlie gave us in our meal planning. Hazel was an elegant woman and we wanted to try and impress her with our culinary skills.

We were so excited when she arrived and to be able to share time together. Brandon planned the fish dinner that we would serve. He had an incredible way of presenting food that made the food jump out and say "try me first." The table looked beautiful with fresh flowers from the garden adding a beautiful island floral centerpiece. When I offered Hazel a cocktail she said that she drank beer until 3 pm and it was later than that so a martini would be in order. We all sipped Martinis, ate hors d' oeuvres and smoked a few cigarettes. Brandon and Hazel both smoked slim long cigarettes that gave them both a silent bit of sophistication as they lit up. Hazel's stories of her time in Hawaii and of her many lives with several husbands were fascinating. She was comfortable with her own soul and her strengths were contagious. After a wonderful evening, we walked her out to her large white Lincoln Continental car. The front and the back door both opened from the middle exposing the large white leather interior. As she drove away, I felt like I was in Hollywood watching a film star heading into the sunset.

I spent as much time as possible out in the gardens that Earl and Dawn had created. The front gardens had a trellis of bright red bougainvillea one either side of the gate. The plants had joined together and created an arbor to walk under when entering through the gate. There was a wide variety of tropical plants, lantana, anthurium, bird of paradise, and ferns. Hanging from a large pine was a *pele's* hair fern flowing gently to the ground. The fern resembled thin strands of volcanic glass stretching from molten lava. The side yard had a variety of orchids and many different ferns, *Hapu'u* tree fern, Sword fern, and others I could not even begin to name. Behind a short cinder block wall, there were banana and plumeria trees that shadowed a plethora of shade-loving impatiens in all colors. I was in awe of the ability of all of this to grow mostly without having to water. The natural rain flow was sufficient for these plants to survive.

Dawn and Earl both worked long hours at their jobs. Earl was a parts manager at the same auto dealership, Schuman Carriage that

Brandon worked at. Dawn was an executive at the Dillingham Land Corporation. We could see around the house several projects that they had begun but were not quite complete. Brandon and I decided to jump in and finish a few of those tasks that we felt that we could do. We finished painting railings that surrounded the dining room platform and in the kitchen pantry. We bravely picked out wallpaper that we thought that they would enjoy and we applied it to the kitchen walls. We cleaned, rearranged a few pieces of furniture and felt pleased with ourselves. When they arrived home from their vacation they greeted us, walked through the home, and sat down to enjoy a cold beer. We sat with them for a short while listening about their adventures in Mexico. There was no mention of our painting, papering etc. When we got in the car to drive back to Waikiki we both said, shit... I think we may have screwed up taking those privileges that we did with their space. It was never mentioned in other gatherings that we had together.

One Friday evening, we were over visiting with Dawn and Earl and I said to everyone, "I think that we all should go over to Hana for a visit together this weekend. Monday is a holiday and we could spend three nights there with Erleen and her family."

Earl responded, "Yes Chet let's do that, will you get us the tickets? Here is my credit card, I will treat."

"I'll call *Aloha Island Air*," I said. "I will see what I can do."

After a short wait on the line I was able to obtain four seats on the first early morning flight the next day and on the last flight Monday night.

"It must be our lucky day," I said. "We are all set to go."

Dawn piped in, "Who made you two the judge and jury, you didn't even consult with Brandon and I."

Earl said, "Give us a break Dawn we both know how much we all love Hana, I doubt that you and Bran have any objections."

Brandon said, "I am supposed to work the holiday, I am not sure that I can go."

Earl said, "I happen to know the boss and he owes me a couple of favors. Don't worry about the time off. And Dawn, you and I've been talking about securing some land for when we retire and possibly moving to Hana. We can look around while we are there."

That was it! We were set to go on our first family vacation together. Brandon was impressed with how much Earl and I enjoyed each other's company. He said it was a relief to him because he was worried about what his father's reaction be to our fairly obvious relationship. My needing the little pills in my pocket became less and less necessary.

We had a wonderful time in Hana spending time singing, laughing, eating, drinking, and listening. Earl had an infectious laugh that brought everyone together into the love that the family freely shared from their own fountains of joy. The baby Miller beer bottles piled up and everyone appeared to be bathed in the splendor of happiness. Earl decided that what we all needed was a weekend together in Oahu and we could go golfing at the *Makaha* course and stay in one of the guest cottages for a weekend. He turned to me and said, "I think that you could arrange that for us Chet."

"No problem," I said. "I will work on that when we return to Honolulu."

I seemed to have been given a special gift of being a planner. By the following Wednesday, I had secured two cottages at the *Makaha Valley County Club*. Brandon and I drove out to preview the accommodations. The golf course was accented by gorgeous vistas as the course weaved along rolling terrain that was framed by dense trees, ferns, and tropical plants. The vacation rentals were sufficient to sleep everyone in the family that was going to attend. Brandon and I, Tommy and Bonnie, Dawn and Earl, and Erleen; Dado would not be unable to join us. Moana was in the mainland with her family on a military base and would not be able to be there.

I was not a golfer and yet Brandon insisted that I rent some clubs, play along the best I could, and at least drive the golf cart. As we teed off early in the day, I could tell that I was going to be a worse golfer than I had imagined. I missed the ball most of the time altogether, and when I did connect the ball would go far to the right into the other fairway. We all laughed and everyone was in good spirits and the course was so beautiful it didn't matter what one's mood was like—the beauty of the place owned the day. The course had many beautiful peacocks, the males would present their feathers in beautiful elongated tail trains, greeting us as we would pass by their playground. There was almost a silent joy with all of us being together in this paradise of splendor. Our weekend was calm and quiet, it allowed a joining of our spirits that were already firmly intact. There was also something eerie in the feeling that I was having. I had a sense that we may never pass this way again.

We stopped by Chinatown on our way to Kaneohe to buy some *Aku* bone and additional poi. I also wanted to buy some century eggs that I had recently discovered a taste for. The eggs are actually not a century old but they are preserved for a few months. They are soaked in a saline solution, and they are coated with a solution of clay and salt, which can also include ash, lime, and rice hulls. The yokes take on a creamy, cheese-like texture and the whites are transformed into a dark-colored jelly. The *Aku* bone is what is left over after the fish monger takes off the luscious red tuna that will be turned into sashimi. There is a minimal amount of fish left. The bone is then seasoned with Hawaiian salt with red pepper flakes, fried and doused with a bit of soy sauce. I picked up some dried cuttlefish, and some *lihing mui* plumbs to finish off our purchases. An afternoon of eating *puupuu's* and watching football together in Kaneohe was on the agenda.

The preparation for our food was quick and simple. Chopsticks were laid out, some Asian bowls with white rice in the bottom were passed around. We would jump in with our sticks in our hand and hurry to pick the delicious *Aku* from the bone. Some cold baby Miller beers of course helped it all go down smoothly. A bit different I thought than the people in the mainland with their chips and salsa, potato chips and dips. The beer might be somewhat the same. The baby Millers were a desired beer because they stayed cold while drinking them. The volume was about half of a normal beer, it looked a little bit scary like we were consuming a lot more merely by looking at the amount of empty bottles that quickly collected.

Brandon and I went down to visit with Tommy, Bonnie, and *Elua*. We had asked Bonnie and Tommy a few months ago if they would be willing to let *Elua* live with them. We had determined that it was not fair to keep her locked up in our condo when we went to work. Not a good life for a puppy. We did not see her and hear her bark after us as we climbed the stairs down to their home. As we entered we asked where *Elua* was. Bonnie teared up and said that they were so sorry, *Elua* had been hit by a car and she had passed away. Silent sadness consumed our short visit. There was no blame put on anyone, we were all just sad. We cried together on our way back to Waikiki.

Chapter Fifteen
"E NE'E ANA"
moving

Things were going along very well with my work at Deak Perera. I had been promoted to the Manager of the Airport branch and the lingering personnel issues had slipped away. As part of being a manager I was also now eligible for the bonus program. Each office manager was entitled to a portion of the profits earned directly from the branch that they managed. I was fortunate to be a manager of a very busy profitable branch. The day that I was to receive my first bonus check, Manuel summoned Kamuela and I to the main office in Downtown Honolulu. He informed us that the New York City office was transferring him back to the Stanford Connecticut Perera Bank. He was leaving in two weeks and he was going to be taking Suzanne Lee our lead accountant with him. We were both in shock. I was stunned to the point of having some immediate fear regarding what would happen to me. He said that Mr. Don Johns was going to be made the director of the main office that he was going to vacate. I was sickened to hear that news. Don was the sole owner and employee of a local company that would buy and sell currencies from small local companies. It was well known to Kamuela and I that he would buy extremely low and sell extremely high. We felt that he took advantage of those who had very little knowledge of the currency exchange market. I had always felt his shady side whenever he came into our branch. I asked Mr. VanGelderen how he choose Mr. Johns.

He said that he came highly recommended by Kamuela, he was given an interview by Mr. Deak and by the auditor who had just visited our offices. Somehow I felt a bit betrayed by Kamuela, however she certainly had known him much longer than I had. There were many times that I would visit the Waikiki office and he would be sitting inside the office at Kamuela's desk. A strange turn of events to say the least.

Manuel invited Kamuela and her husband Keoni along with Brandon and I to share dinner with he and his wife Marcella on Saturday. We were to meet him at his favorite Waikiki restaurant that I had previously eaten at with Marcella and him. I was happy that I had a couple of days to collect my thoughts about my future in the company and to prepare to bid him *Aloha*. Our dinner was anything but celebratory. We shared stories about our brief time together and the sorrows of moving on. I went home deflated like a ballon that had gotten too hot and lost its buoyancy. The following day Manuel called me at home and he said that he and Marcella had felt remiss that they had not reciprocated having us to their home. I told him that I had not expected that and we felt lucky to have had dinner with him last night. He asked if Brandon and I would please join them at their home at 250 Ohua, for a light dinner on Friday evening. He said the movers would arrive on Sunday and he didn't want to miss the opportunity to share another meal together.

Manuel asked me of my aspirations with the company. I told him that I had dreamt of living in Europe and I thought perhaps that I could work at the BankHaus Deak office in Vienna, Austria in the future. Manuel said that was clearly not out of reach for me. I had already met with Mr. Otto Rothenmund when he came to our offices in Hawaii. I had also been a tour guide of sorts for him and his wife. Manuel said that he had spoken very highly of me.

Manuel said, "I may have a bit of a pull there for you." With all of that in mind, I decided to buy an Austrian 1 Ducat Gold coin as a parting gift for Mr. VanGelderen. I purchased a going away card for him and Marcella and I put the gold coin in a small clear envelope in the card. I said that I hoped to work someday in the country from which this coin was made. As I wrote my farewell, I had to move the card to the side to keep my tears from staining the inside of the card. Mr. VanGelderen had been the single most influential person in my professional life and he taught me about the business, the value of work ethics, and shared with me how to live with passion. He was all of that to me and more.

Brandon and I walked to their apartment just as the sun was setting. We walked along the beach and past the large Banyan Tree that I had promised to meet the three fellow travelers that moved with me to Hawaii in ten years. A small tear formed in my eyes for the pain of loss of those friends that were there with me for only a short time. And now we were walking to say *Aloha* to my boss, my dearest friend, my mentor and the one who I had looked up to from the first day we met. We were greeted with warm kisses to each of our cheeks and a warmth that is fitting of *Aloha*. We shared fine wines, Italian delicacies that had been delivered, and a wonderful camaraderie of stories and visions of our future. Marcella pointed out beautiful works of art that they had collected in their travels around the world. She picked up two wooden 6 X 8 inch blocks that were carved on one side in a pattern and a handle had been whittled into the other side. Marcella said, "We purchased these on a trip to Indonesia, and I would like you to have them."

I said, "No."

She said, "A gift from the heart should never be refused."

I took out my card and I gave it to the two of them. Manual opened the card, picked up the coin and read my words. He stood up and asked me to stand and we held each other as we cried. I felt that this was not just *Aloha*, this was goodbye.

The following week was horrible at work and even worse since I was asked to work at the main office to help train Mr. Don Johns. Manuel and Marcella requested a quiet departure from Hawaii and wanted to travel alone to the airport. My journey in Hawaii felt like it may be in jeopardy.

The Monday after Manuel's departure all staff were invited to a staff meeting at a posh downtown restaurant. All offices were closed so that every staff member could attend. Mr. Johns set out his directions as to how the offices were to be run. He was assuming all responsibilities for the setting of the currency rates for each office and the management bonus program would be administered by him, and the results of the profits would come from all offices earnings collectively. There was no passion, there was no longer a work family, there was him calling the shots. I felt that he figured because we were 11 hours of flight time away from New York, we certainly would not be having many corporate visitors checking in on the Honolulu offices.

When the first quarterly bonus was to be given after Manuel's departure, Kamuela and I were both delivered an envelope by our courier. My jaw dropped when I saw the amount.

I called Kamuela, "Do you think this is a mistake?"

"No," she said. "Under Don's direction the profit margin of the currencies has grown dramatically."

"This feels strange to me," I said.

Kamuela said, "Enjoy it while it lasts."

I drove home to Brandon and I said, "We need to celebrate." We went to dinner and had fine wine and a delicious meal. I said that I thought that now would be the time for he and I to look at buying a condominium on Kaneohe Bay that we had recently looked at as only in a dream. The condos are built in a lush, well-cared-for complex in the heart of Kaneohe sitting directly about Kaneohe bay, each unit complete with an unobstructed view of the ocean.

Brandon said, "Are you sure that we can afford one?"

"Yes with this first bonus check we could put down 10% and apply further bonus checks to the mortgage principle and build our equity quickly."

He said, "I won't be able to sell the Four Paddle to contribute. My mother purchased the condo and I am paying the mortgage for her to be able to live there."

"That's not a problem," I said. "I think that I will qualify for the loan by myself. I know some of the staff at the Bank of Hawaii and the first Hawaiian Bank and I will ask them to whom I should talk to about a mortgage."

Brandon said, "Okay let's go for it, are you sure you want me to tag along."

"What are you talking about, you crazy man."

Off we went to pick out our unit. This was seriously just crazy, when will I wake up from this dream?

Everything went just fine with the preliminary application for the loan. The seller was still in the unit and the escrow would not be able to close for five months. The owner was in the Air Force and he was due to retire and he would be leaving the islands. The bank would give a final approval for the loan and they would keep the downpayment in escrow. We had a 30-day no fault time frame from either party to be able to terminate the contract without penalty. Everything was as it should be.

The next bonus payment came from Mr. Johns in the same fashion, from the company courier. I was dumbfounded by amount of the check. I called Kamuela and I said this cannot be correct. She said just enjoy it. I called Mr. Johns and I asked if I could meet with him to chat about the bonus payment. He said, "Is there a problem?"

I said, "I think that the amounts of the past two bonus payments should be audited, I feel that the amount may be over inflated. Perhaps since the lead accountant Suzanne was is no longer here, errors in the calculations may be happening."

He said, "I suggest you leave all of that up to me and enjoy the profits that we all have worked for."

After I hung up, I decided that I needed to take the rest of the day off and ponder my conversation. I definitely did not run to the bank with the bonus check. It was still early afternoon in New York City. I decided to make a call to the head office and talk to someone that I trusted. I shared my concern for the issues that seemed untoward that may be happening in the Honolulu offices. I was told to sit tight and not have any conversations with Mr. Johns. Two days later, I was called by Mr. Johns to come to the downtown office. Kamuela immediately called me and said that she too had been summoned to the head office. She said, "You know that we are going downtown to get fired."

"What in the hell are you talking about?" I said.

She said, "Mr. Johns called me and he asked me to go along with what was going to happen in the meeting this morning. He said that I had no reason to worry, that I would be called back."

"So you are telling me that he is going to fire us both and that you have a path to being called back? What a horrible smoke screen. I'm sorry I need to hang up now."

I went outside the airport and I hailed a cab to take me downtown. When I walked into the office, all of my friends, my work family, looked away. It felt like everyone was in on this horrible meeting. Kamuela was already sitting at the desk of Mr. Johns. They were not meeting in the privacy of the company conference room. Mr. Johns asked me to have a seat. He handed me a letter on company letter head. The letter read: Effective immediately your employment with Deak Perera is terminated. You are to surrender your company identification, keys, and brief case to Ms. Rosemary Ambrosi. She will give you a signed receipt for the articles. I felt like there had been a bomb go off near by that was sending a deafening blast to my head. Everything and everyone around me was suddenly silent as if suddenly cocooned. I didn't think that I could stand. Mr. Johns and Kamuela had gotten up and they were now sitting in the conference room. I walked over to Rosemary's desk to give her the items that were requested in the letter. It was obvious to me that she had typed the letter and she knew what was going on. Her cheeks had trails of black sliding downward from her eyeliner being washed away with her salient tears.

I walked to a pay phone that was in front of the First Hawaiian Bank. I called Brandon and the minute he answered I began to sob. He kept asking what was wrong and where was I. It took several minutes before I was able to give him my location. He told me to stay right where I was and he would be right there. It seemed like I had just put the receiver back and he was there. He jumped out of the car and he grabbed me and said, "Honey what is wrong?"

I got in his car and I asked him to take me to the airport. I wanted to go out to the office to talk to my staff and to gather my personal belongings. It was obvious when I got to the office that Mr. Johns had already told all of them. I asked to be buzzed in so that I could talk with them. I was told that I was not to be let in the office. Margie handed me a box that they had packed with my personal items. I asked if they were okay? They said we have been told not to talk to you. I had never been treated in such an inhumane and mean way. This all truly cannot be happening to me in Paradise.

I went back out to Brandon's car and we went to a coffee shop to talk. There were more tears than coffee consumed. We arrived home just in time to sit on the *lanai*, hold each other's hand, and watch the beautiful sunset and pray for healing.

I was awake all night trying to figure out what to do. My whole life had been thrown upside down. I decided first thing in the morning that I was going to call New York City and speak to the auditor that had been to our offices in Hawaii. I had his business card that listed his direct number to his office. I introduced myself and asked him if he had received any communication about the situation in Hawaii with myself and Kamuela. He said that Mr. Johns had called him and assured him that all was well in Hawaii. I went into great detail explaining what I felt was a perhaps a fraudulent situation happening at the helm of Mr. Johns. I told him that there had been no explanation for the reasons for my termination other than my questioning Mr. Johns on the large amounts of the bonus payments to himself and the managers, including myself. I told him of Mr. Johns prior business dealings and his methods of creating profits by under valuing currencies when purchasing and over valuing currencies when selling. I did not see that as something that Deak Perera would like to have a reputation for. I asked him to do what is right for the company that I loved and that I've been loyal to and to send someone out to Hawaii for an audit. I also suggested that he have a long conversation with Mr. Manuel VanGelderen concerning the current events in Hawaii. I told him that I knew that Mr. Johns was planning on being out of town soon for a scheduled trip to Guam, which is the former home of his wife. He said that he was aware of that as Mr. Johns had told him that Kamuela was to be in charge while he was gone. That statement sent off a firecracker in my head. My friend and coworker appeared to be part of the reason that I was having to make this call. I told the auditor that he should perhaps not let Kamuela know that he would be coming to Hawaii. I also made the suggestion that perhaps he could bring Suzanne Lee with him as she had been the lead accountant in the office from the opening day of the offices. She would have intimate knowledge of the workings of the accounts. I thanked him for his time and I wished him a good day.

I wished that my good day would start as it should by going to work. That had been stripped away from me. My only thoughts were that there would be a day of reckoning and that my termination would be seen by the Deak Perera executives as an inappropriate action. This company had become my family, my life, my future, and my passion.

I went to the unemployment office to file for benefits. I was told by the clerk that I was not eligible to apply because the cause listed for my termination was not due to no fault on my own. I told the clerk that I had not been given a reason for termination and I gave her a copy of the letter that Mr. Johns gave me. I explained the situation to the clerk and she said that after I receive my official rejection letter that I could apply for a review hearing. I asked her what the timelines were for that and she said it usually takes two to three months to have a hearing scheduled.

I was determined that I was going to be exonerated and that I would be going back to work at Deak Perera. I knew that perhaps it would take time for that to happen. I went back to the unemployment office to apply for work. The work counselor said that most of the openings would be in the tourism industry. I didn't think that pursuing a job with either the Bank of Hawaii or First Hawaiian Bank would be a good idea. The employment counselor did however give me a listing for a job at the American Savings and Loan and a listing for a shoe salesman at Liberty House Hawaii. I was very familiar with Liberty House and I thought that perhaps that would be a fun diversion job for a short time. I called the contact number at Liberty House and I was invited to come directly to the store on Fort Street Mall at 3 pm for an interview the same day. I put on my best *Aloha* attire and I was actually excited to go to the interview. I was a bit stressed about taking the right bus to get there on time.

The interview went well, it was quick and the most important thing they wanted to know was how soon could I start. I said that I had no experience selling shoes and they said the training would be quick and easy. I accepted the job and I would start the following morning at 10 am. I became the newest sales member of the women's shoe department. I was given a few brief pointers about up selling and offering suggestions to the women asking for particular shoes. I was given a few cheesy quotes to memorize; "One Shoe can change your life"—Cinderella. "You can never take too much care over the choice of your shoes"—Christian Dior.

The challenges were immediate when the store doors where opened. My first client was a very attractive Filipino woman. She said that she was looking for an elegant shoe to wear to an event at a Country Club. I brought out no less than 15 pairs of shoes, some of the choices were in several different colors. Along with changing the shoes, she insisted that I give her a new pair of the disposable socks with each pair that she tried on. After over an hour of that process she stood up and said, "Oh I don't think that any of those shoes speak to me today." After restocking the many shoes that she had tried on, similar situations happened during the rest of my shift. I sold one pair of cheap flip flops to a young woman and that was it for the day. I went home and I told Brandon that I didn't think that I could continue on with the job. I didn't want to give a false pretense of making that job a temporary job or career, so I was going to call them and resign. I would not be working there, and they didn't need to bother with giving me a paycheck.

I called first thing in the morning and I received a very dry response from the sales associate who I had worked with. I made another call to the American Savings and Loan HR department to inquire about the advertised opening that I was given at the unemployment office. I had a brief conversation with the human resource manager and she said it would be their pleasure to meet with me. I scheduled an interview for the first thing the following morning.

I so wanted to be positive about the possibility of beginning another career. My heart was telling me that I was lying to myself, however at this point I needed a job. I had not cashed the bonus check that I had been given from Mr. Johns at Deak Perera. I was going to hold out for a follow up from New York and I would ask them if I should cash the check.

I met the Human Resource manager and we had a pleasant interview. I learned that the American Savings Bank was Hawaii's third-largest financial institution and a subsidiary of the Hawaiian Electric company. There were 55 branches in the islands with several openings. I was offered a job at their main office in downtown Honolulu on King Street. It was strange to be going downtown on the same bus to a street very close to Deak Perera. I was careful not to look towards the direction of the offices that I missed and yet I had tremendous feelings of angst towards.

I met the branch manager and he introduced me to several of his associates. He said that my training would be at the Savings & Loan headquarters two blocks away on the 24th floor. I felt an instant rush of panic, how was I going to be able to ride the elevator and attend the training that was going to be two weeks long. He said that for the day I would be shadowing one of the tellers to get a feel for the type of daily transactions that they processed. I had a hard time focusing on my environment, all I could think of was the elevator. On my half hour lunch I went to the same pay phone that I had called Brandon on a few days ago. I called Dr. Styonovich's office. I told his receptionist that I had a semi-emergency and asked when I could see him. She put me on hold for quite a while and the doctors voice answered. I told him briefly of my dilemma and he said that he was preparing for a conference and that he didn't have any scheduled appointments, he would see me after my work day ended.

"Thank you so much for seeing me on such short notice today Dr. Styonovich."

He replied, "There is no problem, in my profession these types of issues occur more that you would think. I am happy that I had the time for you today, what is your issue?"

I said, "The short answer is that I was offered a job today and the training will take place on the 24th floor of the American Savings Bank tower. As you are aware I have a terrific fear of elevators. I have my valium in my pocket but I don't think that will suffice to get me through this."

He said, "I have used a technique with another client that we can try to get you through this. We will figure out a safety kit for you to take with you when you are in the elevator."

"First you will need a small backpack that is easily accessible. Put a flashlight with a bright luminous light inside, next add a deck of playing cards, a small bottle of water, your favorite snack, a pornographic magazine, a book that you are reading, and your valium. Take this with you and know that this backpack will keep you safe. Always use the restroom before you enter the elevator. Know that you will always be safe with this on your back."

I said, "I am not crazy about carrying around another thing in addition to my valium, but I will definitely give it a try."

"You will be fine Chet, you are much stronger than you give yourself credit for. Focus on your training and lets' meet in one week at the same time."

"Thanks again for seeing me, I will see you next week."

I gathered all of the products necessary including the pornographic magazine. I had to go into one of the seedy adult book stores on Hotel street to buy it. I looked both directions when I entered the book store to make sure nobody I knew would see me. All I saw in each direction were mostly Chinese walking about in China town minding their own business. How crazy was that I thought, as I handed my selection to the clerk. I bought a magazine that was intended for heterosexual individuals, I certainly couldn't have a gay magazine in my backpack what if someone needed to look inside other than me.

I went into the office building early to observe the individuals that were riding elevators. I watched them all and I thought they are all so brave. I decided that I definitely would not be riding the elevator alone, and I also would not be riding it with a large group either. I jumped at the chance to ride with three other individuals. With a slim stroke of luck, one of the occupants was going to the same floor as me. I survived and tried my hardest to relax. When it was time for a lunch break from the training I was asked to go with a small group to get food. I declined stating that I had brought my lunch with me. I sat in the conference room and I ate the snack I had brought and I read the book that was in my backpack. There was no way that I would be taking an elevator up or down more than once each day.

At the end of the two-week training I had survived without having to take a valium. I did not survive the anxieties, I felt them build daily upon each other like building blocks. The management team decided to offer me an administrative position in their foreign currency department in the Bank Tower. I asked where I would be working and they said on the 22nd floor of the same building that I had been training in. I immediately started speaking. "I am sorry I have a debilitating fear of elevators and I cannot accept that position. I thank you for that opportunity, however is there another position that would be open on the main floor of one of the branch offices?"

If they had any criticism of my phobia, it was certainly not displayed. The manager said, "Yes there is an opening as a beginning teller at the Waikiki branch of our Savings & Loan Company on Kuhio Avenue."

I almost blurted out, "I will take it, I have walked past that office many times on Seaside Avenue on my way to the beach, it is a perfect location for me to work."

I fit in well with the staff and the differences between regular banking and savings & loan transactions were minimal. I enjoyed walking to work, and yet I was almost lonesome for my fellow passengers on the bus. I simply was not happy, my spirit was broken, I was feeling lost without my Deak Perera work family.

Three weeks into my employment, I received a call from Deak Perera New York asking if I could attend a meeting at the downtown Honolulu with Mr. Robert Meir, the acting director of Deak Perera Honlulu on the upcoming Friday. I said yes without even considering asking for time off from the Savings and Loan. There would be nothing that would stop me from being here.

The meeting was set for 10 am. I purchased a tailored white shirt, dark blue slacks, blue striped tie, and black oxfords specifically for this meeting. Mr. Meir greeted me with a warm hand shake and he escorted me toward the conference room. Rosemary came over to me and gave me a hug and said it is so good to see you. I was introduced to two middle-aged gentleman who verbally gave me their credentials. They were hired from an independent agency to perform and audit of the Deak Perera offices transactions over the past two years. They asked me specific questions about certain transactions and they asked me if at any time I had any input into the daily setting of the currency rates. I had not, if at any time had I participated in the calculations of the bonus amounts that were paid out to the managers, I had not. Their findings were sent to Mr. Nicholas Deak and Mr. Don Johns had been terminated and could not be located. There was a warrant out for his arrest. It had been assumed that he had taken what he thought was his and left for Guam. With that explanation I was thanked for coming and Mr. Meir escorted me out to the front office. He told me to stay strong and that he would be in touch with me very soon.

The very next day, I received a call at home from a Mr. Ramos from the American Foreign Exchange office in Los Angeles, California. Mr. Ramos said that he had been made aware of what happened to me with Deak Perera. He said that Barbara Taira from the Los Angeles Deak Perera office had called him. She was a personal friend and she had suggested to Mr. Ramos that he hire me to run one of his Los Angeles satellite offices. I told him that I was flattered by his telephone call. I explained to him that I presently had a job with American Savings & Loan. He said that he would like to send me a ticket to fly to Los Angeles on the redeye flight Friday night and we could meet on Saturday morning in their offices on Figueroa. He would arrange a return flight on Sunday to get me back to Honolulu for work on Monday. He would also secure a room for me at the Westin Bonaventure Hotel. Without even thinking, I said yes.

I could hardly wait for Brandon to come home. I was ironing my clothes to take on my trip to Los Angeles when he arrived. I told him the details of my meeting at Deak and of my telephone call with Ramos and of my upcoming trip to Los Angeles. I said to Brandon, what happens if Ramos offers me a job that I don't think that I can refuse? Brandon said, "That's no problem I will just move with you." I almost fell to the floor in joy. This man was willing to follow me from this beautiful island to the mainland, absolutely amazing.

As the giant 747 took off from Honolulu that Friday night I was not excited for the possibilities that may be ahead of me, I was saddened at what I may leave behind. A song written by *Keola Beamer* was playing in my head,

> "Lookin out upon the city lights
> And the stars above the ocean
> Got my ticket for the midnight plane
> And it's not easy to leave again
> Took my clothes and put them in my bag
> Tried not to think just yet of leaving
> Looking out into the city night
> It's not easy to leave again"

❈ ❈ ❈ ❈ ❈

The meeting with Ramos went very well and I was impressed with his professionalism. He was ready on the spot to offer me a managerial position at his downtown office. I told him that the past month had been an extreme rollercoaster ride for me. I thanked him for his confidence in me and I said that I would like to have a week to consider his offer. He said that he understood and that he would welcome my call next Friday with my answer.

When I returned to my hotel room, I had a message on the answering machine from Mr. Thomas Kelly the manager of the Deak Perera office on Figueroa Street in Los Angeles, which was only three blocks from my hotel. Mr. Kelly's message said that he and his staff were in the office today performing inventory. He asked if would come by and introduce myself to him and his staff. The invitation was exciting and yet I had a bit of resistance to accept and walk down to their offices. I decided at least I could walk by the building and take a look. The offices were located on the main floor of the Los Angeles Hilton Hotel. The bellman opened the double doors of the hotel for me, I entered and I peered into the Deak Perera offices which were directly to the left of the hotel entrance. I must have stood a bit longer than a passerby. Mr. Kelly looked up at the door, opened it and said, "Are you Chet?" He said that he recognized me when I entered the hotel from a picture he had seen in the Deak Perera newsletter a couple of months ago.

I was introduced to the staff: Lydia, Yves, George, Helen, and mama Nova. Mama Novas' sister Barbara had previously worked at the Deak offices in Honolulu and now she worked for American Foreign Exchange in Los Angeles. That answered my question as to how it was known that I was in Los Angeles, interviewing with Ramos and staying at the Bonaventure Hotel.

Mr. Kelly invited me into his office to have a visit. He said, "I received a call from Mr. VanGelderen who happens to be a good friend mine. He gave me an update on what was happening in Hawaii. I was sorry to hear of the chaos that you have been put though. Did Ramos offer you a job."

I said, "Yes he did."

Mr. Kelly said, "I talked to one of the attorneys in the New York office concerning your situation. It appears that you had signed a non-compete clause when you hired on with Deak Perera in Honolulu. You agreed to not directly or indirectly compete with the business of Deak Perera for a three-year period. I would like to offer you a job in the Los Angeles office. We will match Ramos' offer and pay your moving costs."

"I am flattered by your offer Mr. Kelly, however I am nervous about the expenses that Mr. Ramos has spent on bringing me to Los Angeles."

Mr. Kelly said, "Don't worry about that, Deak Perera will reimburse Mr. Ramos for the costs that been incurred. Mr. Ramos will understand your non-compete clause preventing you from accepting his offer."

I said, "I appreciate your offer but my heart and soul are in Hawaii. I would like to talk with the management in New York about the possibility of reclaiming the job that I was incorrectly fired from."

Mr. Kelly said, "I understand, please consider my offer, in the mean time I will ask for help from the legal group in New York City to perhaps get your job back in Honolulu."

I thanked him and said my goodbyes to the rest of the staff in the office.

I had a strange sense of fear that Mr. Ramos would find out that I had been to the Deak Perera offices before I was back on the plane heading home. I went back to the hotel and I immediately packed up and went to the airport three hours early. I decided that I would pen a letter to Mr. Ramos thanking him for the job offer and rejecting the offer based on my non-compete clause. I would mail it to him the first thing Monday morning from Honolulu.

"*Aloha* and welcome to Honolulu, local time is 3:45 pm and the temperature is 82 degrees." Those words said by the PanAm Stewardess were once again music to my ears. As I exited the *Wiki Wiki* bus, Brandon was waiting for me with a beautiful purple double orchid lei. We silently held each other and cried. I think that perhaps that was our first public display of affection for one another. I was back home in the islands, in the arms of the person that I was supposed to be with. There would be no job in the mainland that would pry me away from his beautiful scenario. I am where I feel the most alive.

Chapter Sixteen
"MALUHIA"
peaceful

On my first day back to work at the Savings & Loan, I present-ed the Human Resources manager my letter of resignation. I was professional and kind in my wording thanking them for the opportunity that they had given me. I had no trepidation in giving my resignation with no job waiting for me. I had a positive sense that I would be hearing back from the attorney that I had spoken to in the New York City Wall Street headquarters of Deak Perera early on Monday morning before going to work. I had given the Savings and Loan office a two-week notice and hopefully things would begin to fall into place by end of that timeframe. I did not want to focus on the time that I had lost with Deak Perera, I wanted to focus on the worth of the future.

The future quickly was questioned, we were devastated by a tele-phone call from Dawn informing us that Earl had been admitted into the hospital. He had a heart attack and he was scheduled for surgery. Life just seems to blow up and be unkind when least expected. Earl did not survive. There was a severe devastation to the family with Earl's premature death. He was supposed to live out his dream and retire in Hana. I gave Brandon the best support that I knew how by giving him space and quiet time to heal. My words seemed to be so feeble in this most difficult time. I could not comprehend the depth of Brandon's pain. I stood by his side in the darkness and gave him my love and held him close in my arms. His family was very loving and supportive of one another feelings. Their healing and accep-tance of the loss of Earl was a kind and sharing process that let them deal with the realities that come when life ends. The bonds of love in their family that was cultivated by Earl and Dawn gave the family strength to survive. *"E mau loa ana oia iloko o ko kakou naua"*—He will forever be in our hearts.

❀ ❀ ❀ ❀ ❀

A week had past since my last day at the Savings and Loan when I received a very early morning telephone call. It was 10 am in New York City and only 5 am in Honolulu. I was anxious and almost scared to answer the telephone. Bad news always seems to come at odd hours. A woman's voice asked, "Am I speaking to Chet Gritzmacher?"

"Yes," I said. "This is he."

"I am sorry to call you so early in the morning, I wanted to give you time to be able to attend a meeting at the Deak Perera Honolulu, Bishop Street office at 8 am. You have been requested to be in attendance with a member from our legal team and with Mr. Robert C. Meier the Acting Director of the Honolulu office."

I said, "Thank you very much for your call, I will definitely be able to attend the meeting, thank you for the invitation."

"Chet thank you for your patience. I know you have been through a lot. It will all work out."

Those parting words set the path for the day. I put on my best white shirt, striped tie, blue slacks, and my oxfords that I had smartly polished. Brandon said that he would take me to the office so that I didn't have to take the bus.

Everything seemed to be going backwards. The hunched over Japanese woman was out in front of the Four Paddle picking up the rubber tree leaves that had fallen, the busses were making their way into the city, the morning paddlers were completing their morning exercises, and all of the early risers were exercising in the Ala Moana Park. There was so much visual joy happening, the beauty was a reminder to myself to let nothing steal my joy or kill my peace. That reminder was easier to keep in mind while living in this most beautiful paradise of Hawaii.

I went into the meeting with a sense that nothing could ruin this most perfect day. I was invited into the conference room. The other staff members were not yet in the office. Mr. Meir shook my hand and he introduced me to Mr. Jorge Freddy who was a labor and employment attorney. He had flown in from New York City for this meeting. Mr. Meir began by saying that he was sorry for all that had happened and that my termination was without merit. He also said that there were legal proceedings in place against Mr. Don Johns, but the details were privileged. He went on to say that there had been a staff meeting with all of the employees in the Hawaii Deak Perera offices briefing them of the events. Mr. Meir said I am pleased to offer you the position of the Manager of the Airport office that you previously occupied. Mr. Freddy continued with an apology on behalf of Deak Perera. He said that having been wrongly terminated, I was entitled to a full renewal of benefits and wages. He said that my retirement benefits and my back wages would be given to me in a lump sum. If I agreed to the terms I would need to sign a document that would state that I would not pursue any other wrongful termination actions. I asked to have some time to read over the documents before I would sign.

Mr. Freddy said, "Of course take your time, Mr. Meir and I will leave you to carefully read the documents while we go find a fresh cup of coffee."

They came back in an hour or so, I handed the document to Mr. Freddy that I had already signed. I said, "I have one other issue to discuss. I have the last bonus check that I was given by Mr. Johns that I have not cashed." Mr. Freddy said, "I think you have utmost integrity. That check is yours, you earned it and you deserve it."

I was officially back where I should be with my Deak Perera family. The relief and joy that I felt truly had no description, it was indescribable.

Brandon and I went to dinner that night and shared a peaceful loving time reflecting on all that had taken place. The joys of each other, the joy of having my job, and the beautiful remembrances that we had in our hearts of wonderful times with Earl. We talked about the Escrow for the purchase of *Puu Alii* that was soon coming due. I told Brandon that perhaps we should cancel the Escrow and revisit the purchase at some time in the future. We had several conversations over the past several months about the possibility of both of us pursuing further education. I had told Brandon that I often thought of completing my degree. Brandon was a very good multimedia artist. He expressed an interest in attending a University to fine tune his skills. I loved that were living in the moment, yet we had our feet going forward into the future. We would keep my bonus check and my lump sum salary payments in an account to be used for future education.

Everything at work seemed to be right back where it had begun. Kamuela was no longer working at Deak Perera, she was now an Executive with the Outrigger Hotel group. We met for lunch and I was relieved to hear that my assumptions as to the proceedings that had taken place with her and Mr. Johns were incorrect. She too had been devastated, she had a close friendship and a trust in him. Our meeting was very healing, she was a beautiful person and I had missed her local girl energies.

We decided that we needed a quiet weekend on the Windward side. We drove over to Kaneohe using the *Likelike* Highway instead of the *Pali* Highway. The *Likelike* is one of three main highways that passes through the *Ko'olau* Mountains. The highway passes through the mountains using the two independent Wilson Tunnels that are each half a mile long. The views of Kaheohe bay from the highway are simply outstanding. As the Highway reaches the city there is a botanical garden called *Ho'omaluhia*. To be at peace. There are 400 acres of lush acreage with trails along a picturesque lake and walking trails. We decided to enter the park and spend some time to enjoy the splendor of the day. We were early and it was a perfect time to just be with one another. We walked mostly in silence, I was comfortable with the person that I loved and silence was at is best when we were together. We continued on to Dawn's home that was only a few minutes drive away.

Dawn was in the kitchen mixing poi, she welcomed us to grab a cold beer from the outdoor fridge. She had purchased some fresh *Aku* and she asked Brandon to do the honors and slice the fish. We had a simple lunch with fish, poi, rice, daikon radish, and kimchee. She wanted to talk to us about the possibilities of us moving into her home. She said that she wanted to have a change of scenery and that she would be moving into the Ala Moana area in a high-rise apartment. She said that she was wanting to be able to walk to work and not have to drive in the traffic. Brandon and I looked at each other and we both knew the answer, a definite yes. We had stayed here before when she and Earl were on vacation and we loved our time there. Dawn said that she would handle listing the Four Paddle as a rental. We agreed that we would move in at the end of the month. We would not move any furniture, the Four Paddle condo would be rented as a furnished unit, and Dawn was going to equip her unit with all new furnishings. Dawn asked if we would accompany her to Sonny and Randy's house for a Sunday brunch, and we gladly agreed.

We traveled to their home that was located directly on the beach side of the ocean in Hawaii Kai. I had not met Sonny, she was not at the Willows when we were there with Hazel. The home was a large white elegant flowing home, floor to ceiling windows and a welcoming seaside patio bid us welcome. Sonny greeted us, welcomed us, and thanked us for coming. She looked stunning with her dark flowing hair that had been pulled back into a subtle but elegant bun style. She was wearing a white flowing gown and her wrists were wrapped with several gold Hawaiian bracelets. Randy greeted us briefly as he made his way to greet his other guests. Our drinks were served to us by handsome young men carrying silver platters filled with tall glasses of white wine. I am sure that was by design since the carpet was a brilliant white, red wine would not have done well with any accidental spillage. Hazel was dressed in a long speckled formal dress that was beautiful shade of blue. The bay that the home was located on was a very shallow inlet, the tide was out and it was a reminder that life's low tides allow time to appreciate the hidden beauty beneath the surface. It was definitely a beauty to behold.

Brandon and I seemed to have achieved a good rhythm with our lives. We made the most of our last month in Waikiki, we never tired of just sitting on the *lanai* and watching the sunsets. I had disposed of my baggies of Marijuana and I had not shared that part of myself with Brandon. It was a bit ironic; we had visited a relative that had a pig farm in the lush jungle outside of Kaneohe. I had admired a very unique plant that was growing around the pigsty in abundance. It wasn't until we were home that Brandon had said that the plants were marijuana. He said that there was a good market for marijuana in Hawaii. Neither one of us mentioned using any of the plant for pleasure. Just a few weeks after we had visited the pig farm the news announced that Operation Greenharvest had begun on the Big Island of Hawaii. The operation was a joint effort with federal, state, and local narcotics officers. Low flying helicopters would survey the land to locate marijuana farms. There was an amnesty announced that allowed residents to turn in or destroy their crops. The penalties were stiff for being caught for commercially growing marijuana, your property would be taken and your land would be given to the State. I never returned to the pig farm to see if the stash of beautiful plants had been destroyed.

The end of the month brought lots of movements in Brandon's family. We moved into Dawns home, she moved into the city, Bonnie and Tommy moved into a new condo that was alongside a condo that was occupied by Moana and Randy. The condos were located near the beautiful Valley of the Temples Memorial Park, Cemetery

and crematorium. The Park was at the foot of the Ko'olau mountains, near the town of Kaneohe. Thousands of Buddhist, Shinto,
Protestant and Catholic residents of Hawaii are buried there. It was
also the final resting place for Earl.

❀ ❀ ❀ ❀ ❀

I read the story of Father Damien and the plight of the lepers in
Molokai, it piqued an interest in my wanting to go there. We were in
Kaneohe visiting and I shared with Tommy and Bonnie my interest
in the Leper Colony. Tommy said that a cousin of his was involved
in the business that took tourists down to the colony on Mules. He
said that he would give a call to his cousin to see if there would be
space for Brandon and I to go with them on Mules to Kalaupapa. As
it is with most things in my life that happen quickly, we were signed
up for a trip down to the colony the following weekend. That would
work out perfectly as it was the week prior to our move to Kaneohe.
I booked us a flight late on Friday afternoon, a rental car, a hotel for
three nights and a return flight first thing on Monday morning.

We arrived as the early morning mist was still filtering through
the trees surrounding the mule stables. We were matched to a particular mule based on our size and weight. We were each introduced to mule and we learned its name and the names of our Mule
Skinners. The skinners gave us a briefing on how to ride and control
our mules. We were off for our ride down to Kalaupapa located 1,700
feet below along the most spectacular and highest sea cliffs in the
world. We traversed down the 2.9 mile trail that had 26 switchbacks
and beautiful but scary views of the coastline below. Most of the people on the trek down were absolutely speechless, including myself.
When we reached the bottom we were met by our leper tour guides.
We experienced the most remarkable tour of their community that
had been hidden away for so many years. We learned of the leper
colony, its people, the incredible tales of struggle and human suf-
fering along with stories of courage and love. We visited the grave

site of Father Damien, the historic Belgium Priest who loved and served this colony of outcasts. We visited his church and then we enjoyed lunch at a park that overlooked the sea cliffs and waterfalls. The lunch had been prepared by the lepers, and I have to be honest that I had a wee bit of angst in eating the sandwiches. The ride back up was equally as spectacular and I knew that this day would be a memory that I would never forget.

Molokai is a small island that is only 10 miles wide and 38 miles long. The island is peaceful and felt like an island that had not changed much to accommodate tourism. That was a good thing for us, we appreciated exploring the island without buses full of people. The island of Molokai is known as the "Friendly Isle" and visiting the island slows one down, there are very few automobiles and there is not one single traffic light on the island. We stayed at a small bed and breakfast in *Kaunakakai*. We sat on the beach and we reflected on our blessings and gave our thoughts and well wishes to the lepers and their struggles and survival on this quiet island.

❈ ❈ ❈ ❈ ❈

It was time for us to begin our moving process to Kaneohe. I certainly did not have much to move. I had my bicycle and a limited amount of clothing. Brandon was leaving all of his furnishing there so we had everything moved in just two carloads. Brandon arranged to have the apartment fumigated because of the plethora of cockroaches that love to live in the warmth behind the refrigerator and in the corners of all of the cupboards. I thought that it was strange that there we so many in a building that was 100% cement.

I had recently received letters from my mother's sister Annie in Salt Lake City and from my fathers sister Aunt Vera in Minnesota, I needed to respond with my new address. Their letters always touched me knowing that they took their time to correspond with me. I would have loved it if they would have had the opportunity to visit with me.

Moving to Kaneohe was bittersweet for me. I had enjoyed so much during my time in Waikiki. So many wonderful experiences and also the heartache of losing friends. I decided that I had to look on the happy side of having had three other people that had fulfilled their wanderlust by moving to Hawaii together with me. I did not say goodbye to them nor did I even see them. It seemed strange to be living just two floors directly above one another yet our paths did not cross, I was saddened by that. I wrote to the landlord that I had signed a year's lease with to explain that I was no longer occupying the condo and I gave her the names of Jackie and Paul and I kindly requested that she reach out to them to transfer the name on the lease to one or both of them. I gave her permission to reassign the lease out of my name.

We helped Dawn move into her apartment on the 17th floor of a high rise condo building. After our first ride up to her unit in one of three small elevators I knew that I would definitely not be visiting her often. The views from her *lanai* were spectacular spanning all the way from the airport down to Diamond Head. I did not spend but a few minutes on her *lanai*, I started to experience vertigo and acrophobia at the same time, I thought what if the door closed and locked behind me what would I do. I backed slowly back into the safety of the inside of her dining room. Dawn had furnished her condo in true island style. Her furniture was wicker with white and yellow cushions. It was a very happy and cheery space. She said that she was excited to experience this type of living and it would give her the opportunity to close the door and take a cruise which is something that she had been wanting to do. I thanked her for the opportunity to live in her home, we would take good care of it and we would look forward to her visits.

Pulling up to our home on Kahiko Street it felt so familiar. I had that sensation that I had lived here perhaps in another life time. Brandon and I had visions of completing a few upgrades to the home and making it feel like our own space. My special interest was in the gardens. I had ideas of growing more fruits and vegetables amongst the flora and fauna around the house. I was definitely going to ask the Japanese man down the street if I could have some of his papaya tree starts that were growing on the asphalt across the street from his yard. Gladys and Charlie saw me out in the front yard and brought over another large bag of avocados. The said that it had been an adjustment for them seeing everyone leave the Fernandez home. The death of Earl had been very hard on them. They said they understood Dawns need to move into the city and move forward with her life.

Chapter Seventeen
"WELINA MAI I KO'U"
welcome to my island

I found that living in Dawns home in Kaneohe gave me a jolt of homesickness. I decided that I wanted to call my family and invite them to come and visit Brandon and I. I called my mom and dad and they said that they would ask Kathy to accompany them with her two sons. I was excited to hear that they would consider making the trip. I was aware that with my mother's limited mobility due to her stroke it may be a bit challenging. Surprisingly enough Kathy called me a few days later and said yes, they would love to come. She said that she was working out the details and she would call back soon.

They arrived and I was there waiting for them with leis in hand. It was joyful for me to see them here on my island. I walked them by the Deak Perera offices where I worked and explained just briefly what types of transactions we processed. They were all very tired having flown for over seven hours with a three hour lay over in San Francisco. We went straight to our home in Kaneohe for a rest. I took mom and dad into one of the guest bedrooms. My mom walked to the side of the bed and fell straight backwards to the floor. I freaked out and helped her up. She was not hurt and I was convinced that she simply needed to rest so I helped her into bed. A few minutes later Kathy had gone into the bathroom and she screamed like she was getting stabbed. I ran to see what was causing her trauma and it was one of our dear sweet B52 cockroaches hanging on the door that was freaking her out. In Hawaii, it is said that cockroaches fly like airplanes, the roaches are afraid of rats, rats are afraid of cats, cats are afraid of dogs, man is afraid of woman, and woman is afraid of cockroaches! Those statements clearly held true for Kathy.

I wanted to make the most of their visit, so I took a week's vacation from work to spend the time with them. I had booked trips to Maui and Kauai, Brandon would join us on the trip to Maui.

We started off the following day in a large rental car that would hold all of us to circle the island. We went to the *Pali* Lookout to help give them a perspective of the Windward side and where we were living. Onward we went to downtown Honolulu. My mother marveled at the tall buildings, she had not traveled to a big city in many year's. I drove them by the Deak Perera offices and explained that was where my present career all stated. As we continued on past Ala Moana Park my father wanted to stop and talk to the fisherman who were casting their lines into the sea. He came back to the bench where mother and I were sitting a bit disappointed because he said that he was unable to understand them. Kathy and the boys jumped at the chance to enjoy the beautiful white sandy beach. Before long the boys had Kathy's body buried up to her neck in the fine white sand. The waves along the shore were very light and it allowed Kathy and the boys to enjoy their first dip in the Pacific Ocean. The ocean has a power to stir the heart, inspire the imagination and it brings eternal joy to the soul. I knew that this day will remain in the hearts and minds of Kathy, Sean and Brian for years to come.

The day was beautiful with light trade winds blowing by with white billowy clouds floating above the azure sea. Summer in Honolulu brings the sweet smell of mangos, guava, and passionfruit that is ripe for picking. The streets are arbored with fiery red umbrellas of poinciana trees and pink and white blossoming monkeypod trees. The trade winds prevail all summer long bringing what the old Hawaiians called *makani olu' olu'* "fair wind." The timing was perfect to share my island paradise with my family.

Kathy's small boys Sean and Brian were becoming a bit antsy in the car so it was time to stop and let them roam a bit. We stopped at the *Kahuku* Sugar Mill that had ceased operations as a working sugar mill a couple of years back. We walked around the mill viewing the large gears and old machinery that would have milled the sugar. We took turns taking each others pictures behind the placards of a beach boy and beach girl whose heads were cut out so that we could stand behind and place our faces in the cutouts. We purchased some local shave ice to help us cool down on the hot humid day. A sure way to live *Aloha* is to have a local shave ice cone that is lathered with pineapple, coconut, passion fruit, peach, hawaiian punch or strawberry syrup. The fine fluffy ice looks like real snow in a cup, a large block of ice is shaved finely to produce the perfect frozen delicacy.

We continued on to watch a few surfers along the north shore. The summer months waves are less consistent with smaller swells, there were many locals catching a small wave and riding it to the shore. We stopped for lunch at a restaurant across from Waimea bay and enjoyed eating some local *Mahi Mahi* and watching the surfers on the sea.

The Polynesian Cultural Center was halfway on our circle island tour. We were able to buy tickets for the early show and have some time to explore the villages along the river. The show provided a stunning presentation, with many Polynesian natives performing their talented gifts from each of the Islands that they represented. The island nations of Tonga, Tahiti, Fiji, Samoa, and Hawaii were all showcased with their native music and dance. The excitement held to the very end with a volcano spurting out steam and fireworks to end the performance.

We had packed a lot into the day but I felt that we must stop for a short visit at the Dole Pineapple plantation. Pineapple fields lined both sides of the highway as we drove on the interior of the island. Dole Pineapple had a commercial fruit stand that was adjacent to one of the fields. We stopped to view the growing pineapples and to purchase and sample some of the sweet fruit straight from the field. We arrived back home to have some time to relax and to get ready to depart for the garden island of Kaui the next morning.

I was very concerned with getting mom on and off from the small inter-island planes. I called Hawaiian airlines and they said that they were well equipped to handle passengers that could not climb up the stairs to board. We arrived early for our departure and the attendant said that they would call us up prior to general boarding to get her on board. Mom was in a wheelchair that was pushed onto a platform, the chair was secured, the worker and she were raised up to the level of the entrance of the airplane. The process was fast and very easy. We all sat in the first rows of the plane and when we landed the same procedure was applied but in reverse after all of the passengers had deplaned.

I had previously been to Kauai with Shawna so I had a fairly good idea of the lay of the land. We were staying at the Kaui Beach club that was located just minutes from the Lihue airport. The resort setting was perfect to settle in and enjoy the ambiance, service and the atmosphere of the quiet resort. The beautiful *Kalapaki* Beach was within steps of the hotel which made easy access for the boys to play on the white sandy beaches. Mom, dad, and I spent most of the time relaxing on the *lanai* and watching the other visiting tourists lounging and swimming at the pools. We were all fascinated by watching the local gardeners as they climbed to the very top of the tall coconut trees to cut off any coconuts that were growing. The gardeners had no ropes or safety nets. Their bare feet took them to the top with a bag that was attached to their backs to fill with the cut coconuts. We learned that the fruits were cut for the safety of the guests to not be hit with falling coconuts. I felt so blessed to have my family visiting, it was something that I thought I could only dream about and it was happening. My mother's determination to not let her handicap stop her from enjoying life was admirable. We were experiencing kindness and love with helpful local residents everywhere that we had been. The next day, we boarded a river boat to take us two miles up the *Wailua* River to the famous Fern Grotto. At the Fern Grotto landing we took a short nature walk through the lush rainforest to the exotic Grotto. A trio of performers sang to us the Hawaiian Wedding

Song as we all teared up at the beauty of this moment. Along the way back we learned that the *Wailua* River is the only navigable river in all of the Hawaiian Islands. The tropical landscapes passing by along the calm river that made its way to the sea were adding an abundance of joy to our hearts. The melodic Hawaiian music was in harmony with the landscapes of the moment. We would leave Kaui the following morning with joyful memories of the tropical paradise that had surrounded our souls.

Our next stop on our inter-island adventure was the Valley Isle of Maui. We were fortunate to be able to stay in one of the rental units that Dawn owned directly across the street from Makena Beach. The boys had a great time enjoying the sand and the quiet waves rolling in from the bay. We decided to stay at the condo all day and recuperate from the stressors of the inter-island flight and the short drive to the condo. Brandon was along for this trip and he agreed to cook us dinner. Brandon's dinners were always a work of art and it would give my family time to get to know him better. Brandon suggested that we travel the long road to Hana the following day, his sister lived there and we would all have the opportunity to meet her and her family and share in some of the local flavor of the town of Hana.

We left the condo early to take our time for the 65-mile trek each way. Brandon said that it would take 10 to 12 hours taking our time to enjoy the views and not get dizzy from all of the switch backs. It was indeed a long drive, Brandon pulled off the road several times for us to stretch and have a beverage. Brandon's sister Erleen was working at the Medical Clinic in Hana so we were only able to visit for a short time. We went to the Hana Store to meet her husband Dado and buy a few snacks to keep us happy for the long ride back to our condo. We had about an hour of travel in the dark before getting back. We were all happy that we had another day in Maui the following day before heading back to Kaneohe.

It was harder to say goodbye to my family when they left me to go back to Utah than it was for me so say goodbye to them when I left for Hawaii. I thought how lucky I was to have them come visit me, it made saying goodbye so difficult. I had a sense in my heart that the once-in-a- lifetime opportunity for them to come to Hawaii to visit me was over. I was comforted in my heart to know that this *Aloha* to them was not forever, not the end, it simply meant I will miss you until we meet again.

I called Dawn the following day to thank her for giving us the opportunity for my family to stay in her home and for the days of stay in Maui. I invited her to come over for dinner with us on Saturday. She said that she had a prior obligation that she would like to offer us to attend with her. She had a friend that lived in Pearl City and she was having a gathering of her spiritual friends to make rosaries and prayer beads in her garden. There would be a Marian devotion of the Rosary with some singing and prayers and a recitation of the Hail Mary.

The home was located at the top of a small ridge with a panoramic view from the North of Makaha, Barbers Point, Pearl Harbor, Honolulu International Airport, Ewa Beach, The Pink buildings of Tripler Army Hospital and onward to Waikiki and Diamond Head. We were greeted by a lovely Hawaiian elderly woman with a lei that she adorned on each of us. We were welcomed to the peaceful gathering with a basket of beads twine and flowers. We joined a dozen or so other Hawaiian women who were sitting on the manicured lawn. We followed along with a short demonstration on how to complete our individualized prayer beads intertwined with flowers. Quiet Hawaiian music was being played in the background and it blended gently with the first Hail Mary recitation. The perfect evening ended with a wonderful sunset and a beautiful Hula performed by three of the Hawaiian women in attendance. Our host favored us with her Hula Blessing, *Hau'oli Makahiki Hou*, "May you have grace in your step, song in your hand and *Aloha* in your heart."

Chapter Eighteen

"MAHALO I NA LA"
cherish the days

I was becoming more involved with the different services that Deak Perera offered. I was spending two days a week at the main office working along side Mr. Meier learning of the details of services that I was not aware that we provided. We had a large investment portfolio that we offered to clients that involved trading of currencies and gold. The mystery of how we received clients was never fully answered. One day, a fairly disheveled young man with long hair wearing a tank top and flip flops walked into the office. No one jumped up to help him, so I stepped forward and asked if I could help him. He said yes, but was there somewhere a bit more private that we could talk. I invited him into the conference room and welcomed him to a chair. He said that he was interested in participating in our foreign currency investment portfolio. He said that he was diversifying his wealth and he would like to participate in an investment with Deak Perera in the amount of $350,000. He said that he had that amount in his safe deposit box at First Hawaiian Bank and that he could access it when we had completed the investment contracts. I thanked him for his wanting to participate in the fine Investment Portfolio that Deak Perera offered. I asked him if I could introduce him to Mr. Meier, I said that Mr. Meier could answer detailed questions that he may have. He welcomed the inclusion of Mr. Meir and in three hours time his funds had been delivered, counted, and deposited into the Deak Perera accounts. Mr. Meir said to me, "How did you do that, he looked like someone that couldn't afford a new shirt, let alone a large investment."

I said, "All of the other staff in the office had that same opinion of his possible wealth based on his looks and I was the only one that had not made that judgment call."

Mr. Meier said, "Well I am impressed and I learned something from you today. You handled that transaction with a kind professionalism and it worked, congratulations."

"I appreciate that," I said. "I look forward to more to those types of transactions in the future."

Mr. Meier said I have a couple of clients coming into the office next week. I am going to Switzerland to visit my father for two weeks, and I am putting you in charge while I am gone. One of the clients are parents of a high-profile performer and they like to stay anonymous, their daughter is a pop star on the mainland. Please refrain from any reference to her when you are going over the investment portfolio.

"Thank you for that information," I said. "I will take good care of them, thank you for your trust in me, we have a great staff and all will go well. I'm excited for you to have the opportunity to visit your father, and I assume you will visit our Foreign Commerce Bank while you are there?"

He said, "I am actually staying very clear of there. I worked there for several years and I didn't leave on the best of terms when I left to come to Hawaii. I will leave that up to you when you go to work for Bankhaus Deak in Vienna."

I was stunned by his comment. I did not know that he knew of my ambition to work in Austria. I think I may have a couple of supporters Mr. Meier and Mr. VanGelderen that can perhaps help me make that happen.

We continued on with our training on some of the idiosyncrasies of the business that are more specialized. Fortunately, there were specific staff members that were experts in their field. Gladys Kawelo was an expert in the transitions of money that would be sent to other countries and monies that would come into our office. We had one unnamed gentleman who would come into our office with a suitcase full of currency. He was one of many couriers that I came to know. The monies would be counted by two staff members and the currencies would be purchased by Deak Perera and turned into US Dollars. We would package up currency notes to be sent to various countries. Some of the currencies were being sent to family members outside the United States from field workers and immigrant laborers. Some currencies were sent to countries where it was illegal to exchange their monies for US Dollars, such as China and Russia. Monies to those countries would be packaged as if they contained a gift. The packages would be sent from the Post Office by Certified mail with only the name of the courier as the sender and not the company. The Filipino community would send money on a very regular basis to their families in the Philippine islands. We had a staff member dedicated to those transactions. A Filipino staff member Luzvinda Lanneta handled all of those transactions. A log was kept with the information of the families that would receive the monies and the sender of the currency for follow up if necessary. Most of the clients could not speak English and she would be the only one in the office that could complete these weekly transactions. The workers had tremendous trust in Luzvinda (Elvie) and would hand her envelopes filled with US currency to be converted into Pesos' and sent to their families. They had trust that they were being given a fair conversion and that the transaction would be completed and received by their families in the Philippine Islands. We had a gentleman who would buy up the coins that we had purchased. We always discouraged travelers from bringing back coins from foreign countries. We would offer no more than 40% of their value. The person buying the coins would come into our offices and spend hours separating the coins that he could resale. He would buy those coins for a fraction of their value and he would carry the coins aboard a plane to Canada.

The coins that were 100% silver brought him top dollar and most other coins were exchanged close to the value of the paper currency. We often thought that this person made more money that we did on any of those transactions. We simply did not have the resources to buy and sell coins from other countries. On December 31, 1974 President Gerald Ford signed a bill legalizing private ownership of gold coins and bars. Our company was in position to immediately sell gold coins and bars that we had been purchasing from clients for years. The Vietnamese would sell us gold leaf that was .9999 fine gold. We had a specialist on board who would verify the authenticity and the purity of the gold and purchase it for the company. The South African Krugerrrand was very popular and easy to buy and sell. The Krugerrand was 1 troy ounce of fine gold. It was minted with a copper-gold alloy that made it more durable that pure gold. The Krugerrand counted for 90% of the global coin market, and it was easy to buy and sell the coins to investors. The Krugerrand would require no assay when an owner would buy and sell the coins. All individual transactions were kept to less than $5,000 and therefore no name or reporting was required. It was used as a tax shelter for sophisticated wealthy investors who would buy them and stock pile them in bank safety deposit boxes. There was always a commission paid by the purchaser/seller to Deak Perea regardless of the price of gold for that day. The staff member that was in charge of the gold inventory had to keep a close watch on the fluctuations of the market so as not to have a large amount of inventory in case of a downward market price. The more that I learned the more I became a bit nervous about my temporary position of manager in the absence of Mr. Meier. Everything went well for the couple of weeks that Mr. Meier was gone and I was glad to slide back into my managerial position at the Airport branch.

Deak Perera decided to send all Branch Managers to training with the Dale Carnegie institute. A leadership course was coming to Hawaii and I was enrolled in the class. The course was intended to expand my influence and strengthen relationships with my staff. I would learn to project a confident attitude, communicate logically and clearly to engage my staff as listeners and motivate them to succeed. I would transition from a high performer into an effective and engaging leader. I would learn the tools to build a team that was confident, enthusiastic, and empowered to deliver results. In reading the syllabus, it sounded fairly direct in its approach and I was excited for the opportunity to attend. I was the only attendee from our Hawaii offices. The classes were held daily for two weeks in small conference room of a hotel with 24 participants from a variety of local businesses. I found the course work and the written documentation to be energizing. There were several in-your-face exercises that proved a bit challenging for me. One of the tasks involved me stepping into a crowded elevator as the last person on. I was to face the others in the elevator and not turn around facing the door. I was to look at the passengers and observe their behavior. My first fear was just having to get in a damn elevator and secondly I had to complete the same task at three different times of the day. I was to complete the task in a building that housed several local businesses. I was to ride up when the workers were coming to work, when they were going to lunch and when they were going home. The findings that I reported back to the class were a bit surprising. The first ride of the day was the worst. I saw fear in the other riders, several of the people exhibited body language of wanting to back away from me and watch me the whole time. Others would simply look completely away from me. I had one gentleman ask me, "What do you think you are doing?" I simply said that I was completing an experiment for a class and the relief was immediately apparent on the face of many of the riders. Some riders actually turned partially backward, perhaps with a sensibility and an urge to conform to my stature. No one actually stood backward. Men were more likely to exhibit a visual sense of discomfort, where the women seemed to want to be invisible. The conformity of each of the groups in the elevator stayed the same. The awkwardness of me not being part of the social norm and facing the wrong way was a discomfort for the group, but not enough for anyone to ask me to please turn around. I described my findings to our group and said that I found that I forgot a bit of my fear of riding elevators and replaced it with a fear of the group that I was staring at. I wasn't sure that I was the right candidate for that experiment. I came away from the training with a sense that the training should be offered to all full-time staff members. It would give the company better employee retention and promote that idea that the staff want positive encouragement as well as income. That idea did not have merit in our small company in Hawaii. Most of the staff had been with the company since it inception, they are not likely to leave and the cost of sending everyone to class was prohibitive. I was fortunate to have been able to learn additional skills that would help me in my future professional and personal relations.

Brandon had started to work on new art projects and he began writing a journal as well. His talents were so obvious to me and I felt that he could excel with additional education. We began having conversations of ways that we could make that happen in our life together. Brandon began to look into the community college programs however the art class offerings were very limited and not of interest to him. I began to look at what my future would look like in our company and the limited positions that I could potentially move into. I had begun to form several relationships with the management staff in the mainland with telephone communications dealing with currency tradings between the offices. The Los Angeles office talked about the need to begin planning for another summer Olympics and the ramping up their airport locations. The New York Offices talked about new offices opening up on 42nd Street and Madison Avenues. Our European offices were all very well established banking establishments focusing heavily on foreign investment. I was confident that I could fit into any of those scenarios in my future.

I began to look at the possibilities of returning to the University of Utah for a short return to complete my degree. I requested a class catalogue to be sent to Brandon and I to look at class offerings for the next fall semester. It could not hurt to begin to think forward to where our lives would take us.

As thoughts of not living in Hawaii for a while began to take hold, I began to hold tighter onto my life in Paradise. I had gathered all of the things that begin to cement our lives where we live. I had my car shipped to the islands and I actually found that I enjoyed the convenience but I missed the nostalgia and diversity of my fellow bus riders. I was growing in ways and yet leaving behind a bit of the simplicity of Island life that I so enjoyed. I had gained a new *ohana* that colored my life with joy and acceptance, and I had a renewed sense of nostalgia in missing my mainland family. I was confident that all of the joys in my life would continue but the fabric of that woven quilt of experiences would perhaps change in color and texture of places and times yet to happen.

Mr. Otto Roethenmund, the Vice Chairman of the Deak-Perera group was coming to Hawaii with his wife and I was asked to be their escort while in Hawaii. Mr Roethenmund was an esteemed Swiss finance executive who joined the Deak Perera Group in 1956. He was coming to meet with Mr. Meier and visit with Mr. Van Rouke Lavinsky on the Big Island of Hawaii at the company Anthirium farms. My first thought was that the company should be renting a bigger car than mine to transport he and his wife around. I had a fairly new yellow Ford Mustang with yellow leather interior. It was a very nice car but it was on the small side, and it was only a two door. When I pulled up to the curb at the airport to take them into the city I was actually a bit embarrassed. Mr. Roethenmund said to me that he liked my car and that it looked like me. I thought perhaps that was a good thing, and I apologized for having to have his wife sit in the back seat so that he could stretch his long legs to fit in the front seat. Mr. Roethenmund had been briefed by Mr. VanGelderan of my employment with the company and he was intrigued about my initial meeting with Manuel and convincing him to hire me. He said that I had made quite an impression on Manuel, and I told him that the feeling was mutual. I owed most of what I knew and what I had to offer the company was because of Manuel. I told him that Manuel had set the stage in our Hawaii offices for a professional passionate group of local employees with many diverse backgrounds and nationalities that gave us the personnel that we needed for success.

The Roethenmund's spent their time on Oahu at the luxurious Kahala Hilton. The resort had everything that anyone could want for in a tropical beach resort. I picked Mr. Roethenmund up daily for short visits to our offices and I would return him back to the resort in the afternoon. On the day of their scheduled flight to the Big Island of Hawaii a severe tropical storm came to the Islands. Mrs. Roethenmund was very nervous and she asked me if the inter-island flights were safe. She was in tears as she asked Otto if they could postpone their trip. He told her that they were fine and there would be no issues with their flight. I had empathy for her and I assured her that the airlines would not put them in harms way, and if the flight was canceled I would come back and pick them up.

Their trip went well and they came back in awe of the beautiful Anthurium farms on the Big Island. The next two days I escorted them around the Island for a bit of the tourist view of the Islands. I bid them *Aloha* at he airport with a lei for each of them and said please come visit again soon. Mr. Rothenmund said, "Chet perhaps I will see you in New York or Europe in the future, thank you for your kind hospitality."

Mr. Meier called me and asked me to join him and his wife for dinner at their home in Enchanted Lakes. Mr. Meier had not met

Brandon and I didn't ask if I could invite him to come along. It was nice to see Mr. Meier away from the office. He and his wife and their two young boys greeted me with a warm *Aloha* and welcomed me into their home. Mr. Meier was in a Tee Shirt and shorts and I was impressed at his nice tan. They had a great swimming pool that had views overlooking the Kaneohe bay. I could easily see them all soaking up the sun poolside while working on their tans. We had drinks under the umbrellas surrounding the pool prior to taking off our shoes and sitting at the dining room table. Mr. Meiers wife was Chinese and she served us some of the food she had learned to cook from her family. It was a beautiful feast for the eyes as well as the stomach. While his wife was cleaning up Mr. Meir invited me back out to the pool to enjoy the sunset and an after dinner aperitif.

He said, "I want to thank you for helping to give the Roethenmunds a good visit while in Hawaii. They said that they had appreciated getting to know you a bit and for taking your time to show them the islands." He continued on to say, "Mr. Roethenmund heard from Manuel VanGelderen of my ambitions of wanting to some day work at Bankhaus Deak in Vienna, Austria. Do you still have that ambition now that you seem settled in Hawaii? You are doing a great job as the manager of the airport branch, I would hate to see you go."

I said, "I enjoy living and working in Hawaii very much. I've been thinking of the possibility of completing my degree which is only a few credits shy for graduating. I recently called Manuel VanGelderen in New York, I asked him if it would be appropriate for me ask you for a leave of absence? Manuel said that he did not see a reason for not requesting a leave as long as it did not put the office in a hard ship for its continued operations."

Mr. Meier said, "Do you have a particular time that you think you may want to be doing this?"

"I was thinking of perhaps in September when the fall semester would begin at the University of Utah."

He said, "I don't see why that would be a problem. That is far enough out in the year that you could train an acting manager to step in while you are away. I think you should perhaps give yourself enough time to finish your classes and also to venture over to Vienna to visit Bankhaus Deak and the Foreign Commerce Bank in Switzerland. Oh and you could check in on my father for me while in Geneva."

"That is very kind of you to be supporting of my request. I will think more on the timelines after I have contacted the University. Based on our conversation do you think that it would be out of line to ask for a one year leave of absence?"

"No not in the least, I think you have a lot to accomplish in that time frame. Let me talk with the New York office and see what procedures need to be in place for you to take the leave of absence. I want to make sure that we keep you vested in the retirement plan and insurance. I am thinking that we can somehow incorporate your time in Europe as a business expense to the company."

I said, "I cannot thank you enough for your kindness and your understanding in helping me make these additional dreams come true. I am already living a part of my dream by living in Hawaii and working for Deak Perera, this only creates new visions for my future."

He said, "Thank you for joining my family and me today. We have enjoyed the opportunity to get to know more about you."

I said, "I thank you and I will be forever grateful for this day."

Brandon had gone golfing with his brother-in-law while I was visiting with Mr. Meier and his family. I stopped at the store and I bought a bottle of champagne, two T-bone steaks and two large potatoes, sour cream and cheese. We were going to eat mainland style. I wanted to share the news with Brandon about the possibility of taking a leave of absence and going back to school in Utah. Hopefully, Brandon could begin his art classes there and transfer his credits to the University of Hawaii when we returned. The best part about all of this was that we had time to make decisions about moving, school, travel etc. I hoped that Brandon would want to join me and work together towards a continued education. I had already decided that if he did not want to go with me, I was not going to leave the islands. My life was to be where Brandon was. That statement took a long time for me to even say it to myself. I no longer needed the little pills in my pocket to be secure in myself and who I was. My time in Hawaii had some emotional issues that had cropped up, but those issues never overshadowed my happiness living in Hawaii and with Brandon. We had no labels for each other and our affections for one another. We had respect, confidence, trust, and a deep understanding of love for one another.

Brandon came home and saw the champagne chilling on the ice and he said, "Did you get another big bonus and buy another condo?"

"No, I did get a bonus of an opportunity for us to pursue our educations in Utah should we wish to do that."

Brandon said, "Have you already enrolled in classes at the University?"

"No, I asked Mr. Meier if I could pursue the possibility of a one year leave of absence from Deak Perera and he said yes. I did not commit to anything because I wanted to have this conversation with you."

Brandon said, "What if I don't want you to go?"

I said, "You don't want me to go?"

He said, "I don't want you to go without me!"

Mark Twain said, "To get the full value of joy you must have someone to divide it with." I had found that someone.

We both agreed to take things slow and talk things out before we made a decision to move forward with leaving Hawaii.

On Monday morning I called Mr. Meier to again thank him for the kind hospitality that he and his family shared with me. I also asked him if he would not mention my possibility of taking a leave to any of the other staff members. I told him that I had many things to consider before taking that leap and I felt it best to not have my staff members to be aware of the possibility of me leaving. I had made a mental note to take some time with the people that had been important to me in Hawaii. I called the landlord at the Four Paddle to enquire if she still had Paul and Jackie as tenants. She said that no, Jackie had left the Island along with Paul's sister and boyfriend to return the mainland. Paul had moved to another location but she did not have a forwarding address or telephone number. I called my cousin Rosemary in Kaneohe to catch up and I invited her to lunch at Arthurs on King Street. I was wise enough to know that I should take the bus to meet her. She and I had experienced a couple of occasions that drinking was an issue of overabundance.

She previously had asked me to join her at the top of the Sheraton Waikiki, taking that outside elevator that previously had not reached the top was a concern. I waited for her to arrive at the ground level so that we could ride together. The views were more spectacular than I could have imagined. The turquoise waters along the shores of Waikiki were stunning. The ocean floor was visible exposing the shallow reefs that the surfers were floating above. Yes, I decided the ride up the elevator was worth it. We met with the purpose of Rosemary wanting me to learn to enjoy the drinking of Scotch. To her, it was the sophisticated alcohol that one should drink and it left less of a hangover effect the following day. There is an old Irish Proverb that says, "What Scotch Whiskey will not cure, there is no cure for." Rosemary went on with her quest to make me a believer in the pleasantries of Scotch drinking. The bartender brought a variety of different blending of the Whiskey, all of which I detested. At the end of the night I said to Rosemary look at it this way, you were able to drink two for one, mine and yours. I invited Rosemary to leave her car at the hotel and ride back to Kaneohe with me. I had not consumed but a smidgin of alcohol and she was in no shape to drive home. She agreed and of course her Corvette was safe in the hotel parking garage.

At Arthur's, we were seated in the back of the restaurant in a booth that was upholstered in dark burgundy leather. The restaurant was a local watering hole for the business executives that wanted to have a liquid lunch. It was so dark in the restaurant I felt like I needed a flashlight to read the menu. She said that her husband Mark had dropped her off on his way to the Naval Base. She had gone shopping at Liberty House and she had several bags poised next to her at the end of the booth. She said that Mark was going to pick her up outside of Liberty House at 3 pm. Oh my hell I thought what are we going to talk about over three hours. As it turned out the three hours was not an issue. We shared our inner most secrets in the darkness at Arthurs and those secrets will remain just that, secrets.

I had some healing to do with Kamuela. I called her and she suggested that I come to her home and have dinner with her and Keoni. She lived on a street that for some reason I liked the name of "Nawiliwili Street." We had a great dinner and shared wonderful memories of our times together at Deak Perera and specifically with Manuel VanGelderen. I was taken back when they offered me to share a *Paka Lolo* joint with them. I declined their offer to participate saying that I had not smoked since I had met Brandon. Kamuela said that she was doing very well with the Outrigger Hotel chain and that she was traveling internationally with them. I was happy to hear that from her. I bid them my *Aloha* and headed back to Kaneohe.

I decided that I would take my staff for lunch at the beautiful buffet that was set up at the airports fine dining restaurant. I spoke with Mr. Meier about the event and I told him it would be a team building event that was outside of the office. We would take lunch at 1 pm and close the office for two hours. That timeframe in the afternoon was a good time to close as there were no inbound or outbound international flights. I told our five staff members to invite their spouses or significant others if they wished. There was a quiet hesitance to the beginning of our meal. None of the staff members had brought along a guest, and they casually gathered at the Luau buffet line. The Luau menu was beautifully arranged on bamboo laden tables with arrangements of orchids, hibiscus, birds of paradise and other tropical flowers. Seashells were scattered around the tables on top of palm leaves. A full roasted pig was at the helm of the table. I was not sure how appetizing that was, however its flare added a bit of a traditional Hawaiian style luau. There were platters of Rumaki, Ribs, Shrimp, Roasted Pork, Grilled Fish, Chicken Long Rice, Lomi Lomi Salmon, and of course white Rice and Poi. We sat a circular table and the nervous energy slipped away as the eating began. I had an opportunity to observe them amongst their peers. Phil was a short Filipino man with a great laugh. His right hand pinky finger had a nail that was at least an inch long. He pointed it to the side of his hand as he ate. It is said that a long pinky fingernail is an aide to prosperity. Margie was dressed in a beautiful purple Muumuu. Margie was also Filipino and she and Phil seemed to not have an issue with speaking Tagalog to each other at the table. Margie was brilliant yet she always seemed to have her eye on me with distrust. Yui was a very quiet Japanese woman. Her mannerisms were always presented with a shy politeness. She worked very hard, she had little social interaction with the other staff members. Li Min was a very short Chinese woman with a strong quick voice. She had a wonderful command of several Asian languages, Cantonese, Mandarin, Korean, and Thai. Heide was a strong blonde German woman whose husband was in the Navy. She commanded respect and was direct with her conversations. Her European upbringing had given her six fluent European languages. I often felt a bit inferior amongst my staff and the command of the many languages that they could speak. At Deak Perera most of our clientele were from other countries and as least one of our staff members were able to converse with most of them.

As everyone went back to the dessert table, I placed an envelope with each of their names on their placemats. Margie was the first to pick up her envelope and looked straight at me and said is this our letter of dismissal. I answered back, "Inside is a letter thanking all of you for your hard work and loyalty to our company." Each of you are given your choice of a three-night vacation with a guest on any of the Hawaiian Islands. There is a number listed in the letter of the travel agency that services Deak Perera. They have your names and they are expecting your call. I have put up a calendar in my office, and I only ask that you coordinate your time away from the office at differing times to ensure adequate coverage. There was complete silence from all staff members. It was definitely not the reaction that I was expecting. So much for one of the core messages from the Carnegie Institute "Empower with Reward."

Manuel called me from New York and said, "Ciao Chet. I wanted to let you know that me and Marcella will be moving to Miami. I am going there to facilitate transactions that will be taking place with South American Countries. I will be working out of a small office that will not be opened to the public. Marcella and I are happy to move because we have a daughter that lives in Miami and we are glad to have the opportunity to be closer to her. Besides that, I am ready to get back to a warm humid climate."

"Manuel I am so happy for you and Marcella. I wish you the best of luck, please stay in touch."

The conversation was short and he wished me well wherever my future plans took me. I had an eerie feeling when I hung up as the conversation seemed to have some kind of closure.

The company seemed to be having some kind of transitions. Our small operation in the middle of the Pacific was just going on as normal. We had received memorandums of the pending of the closing of the Banking office in Connecticut and the Deak Perera travel check division would be closing and we would no longer be offering them for sale in our offices. I asked Mr. Meir if we had access to the company overall financial statements. He said no, that we were a privately run company and they were not required to publicly provide financial statements. I asked him if he had any concerns for the overall health of the company and he said no, not in the least.

I sent a letter to the University of Utah admissions office requesting information to enroll in the next year's fall classes. They responded that a fall catalogue would be sent to us three months before the beginning to the fall semester. No formal request to enroll in classes would be required. Brandon and I would talk on a regular basis about attending the University of Utah or enrolling in the University of Hawaii. Both of those options had advantages and disadvantages. We both decided that we did want to further our education. The timing of that happening and the details were still not formulated.

❋ ❋ ❋ ❋ ❋

I wanted to know more about Hawaiian mythology. Brandon had told me the story of the flower with petals that grow in a half-circle, the *Naupaka* is a unique flower found only in Hawaii. It's believed to have blossomed this way as a result of an ill-fated love affair between two students at a hula school in Kauai, where dating was forbidden. One night, a teacher spotted the couple and began chasing them. The girl, Paka, hid in a cave, but was found and killed by the teacher, who then chased the boy, *Nau*, up the mountain and killed him. Later on, the flowers were seen growing at the sites where Paka and Nau were killed, their half-petaled took a symbol of the couple's eternal separation. I asked Brandon if we could have a weekend adventure to the beach and to the mountains to find the flowers and take photos. He said that he would ask his family for the best place to go in the mountains to find the plant, the plants were everywhere on the beachside and they would be easy to find. We had a beautiful day at the beach and we found the flower that we were looking for, we ended the day on top of the *Pali* highway and we found its identical mate. We read a poem honoring the myth when we returned home.

> You are my lei of *Naupaka*
> The soft fragrance of love
> We will always be happy
> The flowers, so fragrant
> Two of us, together forever
> You are my flower
> Touched by dew
> Your gentle eyes
> Radiant, like pearls
> Turn to me, my blossom
> Your beauty, mine to indulge
> (I will) cherish and care for you
> *Naupaka*

The reading of the poem was the ending of a perfect day. Honoring the myths and legends of the Islands gave us both joy in our hearts, and we knew that were truly the two luckiest men on all of the islands.

Brandon had lunch with Dawn the following Monday to catch her up on our thoughts of going back to school. Dawn told him that she fully supported us in wanting to fulfill our educational desires. She said that it would not be a problem for her to move back into her home. She said that she had enjoyed her time living in the condo, she also missed her home in Kaneohe. The timing of our possible departure would work out perfectly for the ending of her lease.

We decided to take another trip to Maui and to explore parts of the island that we had not done so on prior trips, and to visit sites of some myths and legends of that island. Legends are often stories of real people and their historic adventures, and myths often convey the ideas of how things came to be that are attributed to gods and goddesses. In Hawaii, these two forms of storytelling are blended together.

We headed to the *Iao Needle* directly after landing. King Kamehameha clashed with Maui's army in this quest to unite the islands. The *Iao Needle*'s towering emerald peaks provided and excellent lookout point for Maui's army. Even with that advantage King Kamehameha defeated Maui's forces in a ferocious battle. We climbed to the ridge-top lookout to see the incredible views of the valley. We continued on other hiking trails that took us along a spiritual rainforest that took us to waterfalls that were set amongst very lush flora and fauna. The stop at the *Iao Needle* was the perfect way to begin our leisure vacation time on Maui.

We checked into our small hotel in the town of Lahaina. The historic whaling village was once the capital of the Hawaiian Kingdom. It was known as *Lele*, which means "relentless sun" in Hawaiian. We immersed ourselves in the culture of Maui by learning about the ancient mode of seafaring by canoe and we had some of Maui's best seaside luau as we watched the setting sun while listening to the sound of the breaking waves on the beach.

We left our hotel before daybreak to drive to the top of Maui's highest peak Mt. Haleakala to view the sunrise. The massive volcano gave us witness to an orange and red-colored dawn that was set amidst the clouds. The views of the island of Maui at sunrise were breathtaking. We made a slow descent along the slopes of the massive volcano taking time to walk amongst the Silverswords that dotted the ancient lava. We admired their low growing rosettes with silvery hairs and fleshy leaves that grew from the center of the unique plant. The plants live to more than 50 years but bloom only once and die. Seeing several of the plants in bloom gave us pause to realize how special this opportunity was that we were seeing. The species of Silverswords we were viewing are unique to all the world on Maui. We spent our last night in Maui sipping a Mai Tai and reflecting with appreciation of our experience of both the myths and legends of the beautiful Island.

When we returned to Kaneohe, we both had a resolve that we were going to go forward with our plans to attend school in the mainland. I began by formalizing my request of a leave of absence from my employment with Deak Perera. I hand wrote the letter on company letterhead several times before I was satisfied with its content. I was requesting a one year leave of absence to complete classes at the University of Utah and also to have an opportunity to spend time at the offices of Bankhaus Deak in Vienna, Austria as was previously discussed with Mr. Meier. All plans would be off if I was not granted the leave, we would remain as we were, happy to be living and working in Hawaii. I tried to put some of the concepts that I had learned along the way with Deak Perea that if I did not go after what I wanted I would never have it. If I did not ask and attempted a step forward I would always be in the same place. If that same place ended up being the Manager of the airport brand of Deak Perera—so be it.

Brandon started spending more time golfing with his friend Chuck. He and his wife were finishing their time commitment in the military and they would be moving back to Wisconsin in the fall. After a few beers in the club house he would come home happy for having the time to catch up with his friend and play golf together, a game they both loved and they were good at.

I decided to try my hand at playing golf to be able to tag along with Brandon at the various courses that he played. Brandon had an old set of clubs that he meticulously cleaned and put them in a new, easy to carry small bag. I had the minimum amount of clubs necessary that a beginner would need. I went to the golf course in Enchanted Lakes and I took a few lessons with the pro. He said that I needed to spend as much time as I could at the driving range to straighten out my swing and improve the direction of the trajectory of the ball. I would try different ways to address and hit the ball, and not much worked. It didn't matter which way I would face, the ball would go directly to my right. Brandon was very kind to attempt to help straighten things out, the outcome was mostly the same. Brandon pointed out to me that if I hit the ball to the right it was called a slice. If I hit the ball to the left it was called a hook, and if I hit it straight it was a miracle!

Tommy and Bonnie were going to go for a visit to Kauai and spend time with their daughter and her family. They suggested that Brandon and I join them on Kauai and they would arrange some Tee times to play The Princeville Golf Course. We didn't have to be asked twice, we jumped on the chance to go back to Kauai. I told Brandon that I was uncertain about playing golf and could I just ride along in the cart. The answer to that was a no, spectators are not allowed on the course, if I was going to be on the course I would need to be golfing.

The Princeville Golf Course is truly one of the world's most stunning golf locations in the world. The immaculate course has six ocean front holes and an amazing "*Aloha* Spirit." The course is perched high about the stunning Hanalei Bay with sleeping views of Kauai's spectacular North Shore. As we walked to the first Tee I looked at the view in front of us and I felt that it surely looked like what I thought heaven would be. The glory of God was clearly proclaimed by the work of his hands in the beauty that was before us.

Brandon, Tommy, and Bonnie were all excellent golfers. I was a nervous wreck, embarrassed and I humiliated myself with my poor performance. I almost laughed when we made it to the Tee on the fourth hole and there was a golf coach that was provided by the course to help with guidance of lining up the drive. He gave us information as to the presence of wind, and the direction that the balls might drift in the present conditions. His being there with us made it all the worse for me. I actually completely missed the ball twice before hitting my famous slice to the right. After we had finished playing the eighteen holes, I still had a tremendous sense of gratitude for being here in this beautiful setting with my wonderful *ohana*.

Being on Kaui gave us pause to look at the island with new sets of eyes, we were uncertain as to when we would have this opportunity again. Before catching a flight home the next day we drove to Waimea Canyon, "The Grand Canyon of the Pacific." Although it is not as big or as old as its Arizona cousin, we would have not encountered anything like its wonder in Hawaii if we had not taken the drive to view it.

Chapter Nineteen

"A HIKI I KO MAKOU HOI ANA MAI"
until we return

The time clock for our pending move seemed to be moving faster than we would have imagined. I needed to look up a quote that I had read about Hawaiian advice to not get a bit overwhelmed.

Lead a colorful life
Breeze through the day
Learn the language of respect
Paddle your own canoe
Share the *Aloha* Spirit
Keep your inner fire burning
Live on Island time!

Life in Hawaii has had some complicated issues, however living on island time had been a breeze.

I received my approval letter for my request for a leave of absence from the New York City office signed by Mr. Leslie Deak. Leslie was the son of Mr. Nicholas Deak the owner and founder of the Deak Perera group. I had not had the privilege of meeting him. He asked me to give him a call when I had my exit dates confirmed to discuss my Bankhaus Deak request. I was blown away that my dream of possibly working in Austria had taken some flight forward. There was a part of me that wanted to say to Leslie that I was disappointed that none of the upper management had given me their support during the most difficult time that I went through because of Mr. Johns. I would try to keep that disappointment to myself.

We received the fall schedule of classes from the University of Utah. Brandon was excited to see several art classes that were available to him without having had completed prior classes. I actually had a tougher decision. My declared major had a couple of classes that I would need to retake. I could perhaps pursue a general studies degree in less time. I called the admissions office and they suggested that I should take a couple of classes that would apply to either of the majors and meet with an advisor when I returned to Utah.

We had sticker shock at total amount of money we needed to send to the University for admissions and for the credit hours that we were to enroll in. It was a bitter reminder of what I had been given and what was paid for with my scholarship. The silver lining was that we had an educational saving account thanks to my bonus payments that I had earned. I had a bit of unfounded regret that we had not gone forward with the purchase of the Condo at *Puu Alii*. That dream will have to be put aside for a future time when we return back home to the islands.

Mr. Meier and I had been having several meetings concerning the management of the Airport office when I left. We came to a mutual decision to offer the job as an opportunity to all of the other Deak Perera offices in the mainland as a one-year temporary reassignment. We were very confident that someone would certainly jump at the opportunity to live in Hawaii and have their living expense paid by the company as well. I worked with the Human Resources office in New York to formulate the details and I provided the information for the summary of duties. The announcement would go out to all offices within the next two weeks. I invited all of my staff to another lunch together, only this time it would be at the airline employee cafeteria. I told them of my impending absence and of the plans of looking for a replacement. I wouldn't say there were a lot of emotions, there were several questions if the other staff members in Hawaii would be eligible to apply. I said that the recruitment would be handled by the Human Resource Department in New York City and that all employees would be welcome to call the office with questions. I stressed to the staff that it would be a temporary advancement until my return after a year of leave. We returned to the office after the lunch with little concern by anyone for the future of the office management. I had another gentle reminder from my Dale Carnegie training, I had confidence in myself that there would be someone to take my place, but no one could replace me. Yes, there was lots of ego in that learned statement, I would be replaced but I would take all of the memories that I had with me.

❀ ❀ ❀ ❀ ❀

Thing started to fall into place for our upcoming move. Brandon made preparations to have his car sent over to the mainland. We were going to try to time the arrival of the car in San Francisco to be able to drive it back to Utah in time for the beginning of the fall semester. We had hopes of packing the car with our personal belongings, but we were told that the car needed to be completely empty. We were not anticipating needing to take much of anything except our clothing and our two Kamaka Ukuleles so that news was ok.

The closer our time came to leaving, the more I seemed to be hanging on to every moment that I could encapsulate in my mind. I relished every day, I stayed complete in my daily routines and I was perhaps a bit cautious of creating new ones.

We had a few additional gatherings on the patio with everyone in our *ohana* to share, beers, pu pu's, stories and most of all their love. The Hawaiian culture teaches their children the value of respect and honor of those older than themselves. Every gathering of the families with the children began with a greeting of honi, honi, "Kisses" and a hello uncle. The children gave space for adult conversations and they were self entertaining, sometimes sitting in the front yard and sharing their voices in song and laughter. The value of *Ho'ohanohano*, "to honor the dignity of others, conduct yourself with distinction, and to cultivate respectfulness" was evident in their teaching from their elders. I, as an adult, was learning that value directly from the actions of the children. At the end of every gathering of the family I was in awe of the joys that were shared and I knew that I was so fortunate to have shared in those joys. The sacred Hawaiian ways came naturally to my *ohana*, *E hele me ka pu'olo*: "Always take an offering with you, make every person place or condition better than you left it, and wherever you go take something with you, this is the way of abundant flow honoring *Ke Akua* (God) and his creation."

❀ ❀ ❀ ❀ ❀

Older traditions in culture between the various nationalities had begun melt away in Hawaii. There had been a nationalist anger in China against mixed race couples marrying that had carried forward to the Chinese that were living in the islands. Slowly the blending of the nationalities was happening. Colleen Chu was going to marry Russell Sato in a very large celebration that I was invited to attend. I had worked along side of Colleen but I had never had a conversation about her personal life. I did notice that she had a very close relationship with Mr. Meir. After I met Mr. Meier's wife who was Chinese, I had made an assumption that perhaps that had been a reason for their bond. When I talked with Colleen about her upcoming marriage, she said that the planning for the marriage had taken over a year. She said that her father initially said that he would not support her marriage to Russell who was a *Katonk*, a mainland-born Japanese. She said that it was only after her father was able to see the strong work ethic, values that Russell had and her strong love for him, that they were given his blessing to go forward. I had never attended such a lavish, formal, affair in my life. Each nationality had wedding traditions and those rituals were blended together into one marriage. As we entered the wedding reception venue, there was a display of the 1000 paper cranes that had been folded that day which signified wishing them 1,000 years of happiness and prosperity. The colors of red and gold played a critical role in all of the Chinese wedding decorations. Red signified love, success, happiness, prosperity, luck, fertility, honor and loyalty, and the gold was a symbol of wealth. I noticed that many of the attendees gave a red packet to the bridesmaid, who I learned would take the packet which contained money and she would record it in a book to be given to the couple after the ceremonies. The traditional Japanese Nuptial cups exchange was performed by the couple. The groom and bride drank sake three times each from three different-sized sake cups called *sakazuki*, symbolically exchanging their marriage vows.

Everyone was seated at an assigned table that had elegant table wear. In traditional Chinese style, the food was placed in the center of each table on the moving platform that would spin around to each place setting. All types of Japanese and Chinese delicacies were continually placed on the tables throughout the meal. The celebration concluded with a money dance in which the bride and groom danced and each guest would pin money onto the gown of the bride. The wishes of each guest were given to the couple for a life of good fortune.

I had learned early on from my first days in Hawaii that the blending of cultures was a significant part of their lives. There may be different religions, different languages, different color of skins, and different traditions but in Hawaii they all became as one in the human race, all of which widens the mind and the spirit. I realized that the cultural differences did not separate me from others, but rather brought me strength in accepting diversity within myself and with others. Perhaps the Psychiatrist Dr. Styonovich knew all along that all I needed was time to absorb the knowledge that the fundamental differences among us were what brings us all together.

❀ ❀ ❀ ❀ ❀

With the details of our departure completed we gave ourselves time to absorb the joy, the love, the warmth and the *Aloha* that we would not leave behind, but we would take with us.

So this was it, it was not an ending but a beginning. Not a good-bye, but a see you later.

"Welcome to San Francisco, local time is 8:45 am and the temperature is 57 degrees. On behalf of Pan-American and the entire crew we bid you a pleasant day and we look forward to seeing you on board again in the near future."

The Hawaiian Star Sirius had guided us safely from Hawaii to our new home in the mainland.

❀ ❀ ❀ ❀ ❀

"In the end we can only regret the chances we didn't take, and the relationships we were afraid to have, and the decisions that we waited to long to make."

Perhaps, I had learned one of the most important lessons of all...

> *"Kahuna Nui Hale Kealohani Makua"*
> Love all you see, including yourself
> *ALOHA*